Return t
&

Hell on Church Street

Charles Dudrey

ISBN: 978-1-60383-362-2

Published by:
Holy Fire Publishing
717 Old Trolley Road
Attn: Suite 6, Publishing Unit #116
Summerville, SC 29485

www.ChristianPublish.com

Cover Design: Jay Cookingham

Editor: Lori Woodward

Printed in the United States of America and the United Kingdom

Book Dedication

This book is dedicated to my lovely wife Diana who through the years has walked beside me in some difficult times and trying situations. She has remained my best friend, steadfast and true, never once passing judgment on me, but instead choosing to encourage me to do what is right. She is the love of my life, my soul mate, and in the depth of my heart she forever remains my Sweetness.

Acknowledgments

Through the years, of my Christian walk there have been many fine people that have loved me and touched my life different in ways. Many have offered me good counsel and have influenced me in making some important life changing decisions. I would like to use this opportunity to mention a few of you. It has been a privilege to know each and every one of you and I continually, thank God for your friendship.

Larry Dublanko:
Thank you pastor, for your leadership and wise council. Both have guided me during the years in my journey with Christ Jesus. Your sound wisdom influenced me in some of the important decisions in my life. You encouraged me through some difficult times and led me on the road to better things. The love and joy I treasure with my wife and family today, is due in a large part because of your guidance.

Edward Casey:
From the first time I met you, I knew that we would be friends. That first Sunday morning seeing you at Oak Hill I recall telling my wife, this man has the love of Christ all over him. My first impression of you has proved to be right. There is no doubt that I was probably a challenge for you at times, however your steadfast love and friendship has never wavered. You

have demonstrated to me over and over again, the love for the brethren.

Danny Simons:
The love and zeal you have for the things of God have been a shining example to me time and time again for years. Your commitment to our friendship has not wavered, and you continue to be steadfast and true to our relationship. God has truly blessed me with the good friend I have in you.

Doug Cotton:
Thank you for sharing with me the vision of what you see God having for His Church, for His people and our community. I want to see things the way you see them, and I want to serve alongside you on the journey. Doug you have been true encouragement to me and you continue to be so. Thank you for being so real, you have inspired me.

William Schmauss:
God has blessed me with the joy of having you as my son. Your loyalty, your love, and your faithfulness to our relationship have been steady and undeniably honorable. I am well pleased to see the man you have chosen to become. I love you.

Prologue

The idea for this book came in three stages. My wife Diana on occasions over the years has suggested that I write a book of my life story. I admit that I have given it some thought myself over the years; however my lack of education and writing skills prevented me from giving the idea any serious consideration.

Then one morning I was visiting with my Pastor who I hadn't known for too long having a cup of coffee. We had been talking and sharing thoughts and our ideas about a wide range of topics when he said, so, tell me your life story Chuck. I thought for a moment, my life story, and then I decided that it would properly be better that he heard it from me first, than from someone else asking him if he knew anything about me. My life to say the least has some ugly history and I haven't always been the kind of man I am today. I do not however make any excuses for anything in my life knowing this, that there continues to be plenty of room for improvement, let there be no doubt. And so I shared with him some of my story and at the end of our conversation he looked at and said "you need to write a book."

That evening sitting at the dinner table my wife asked me how the meeting with the Pastor went. So I shared with her what we had talked about and that, he thinks I should write a book about my life. Well my wife said,

"I have been telling you that for years Chuck, I really think you should too". So I began to ponder this thought and for weeks, one day I would think I would do it and then talk myself out of it. I simply had never written anything and further more; my spelling ability was nonexistent. What would people think about me when they read it, was the big question? Would those that didn't know my history think less of me, and so this went on for a few months.

One Sunday morning we were sitting in Church and our youth pastor was sharing the message. He was sharing with the congregation that there were people in our church that had ideas for inventions that they needed to pursue. He went on to say that someone sitting here probably had a business idea that they had been thinking about for years that they needed to put it into action. He continued to say that God wanted His people to prosper and that is why He gave us these ideas. And when Pastor Wes stated there some people hear that have a story to tell and they need to write a book, I sat up and looked right at him as my wife turned to me and said, see! Well the ride home that afternoon was quiet and uneventful, that in its self is a sure sign, my wife had something to say.

Well sitting at the dinner table once again my wife said, "You know it is no mistake that the Pastor Wes shared that message this morning." Diana I said I don't know where to start and she told me to simply begin with a thought and go from there putting it down on paper. And so we sat there and prayed and asked God to guide and lead me in this writing. I prayed "Father God if this is your will for me to write my story then I will need your help. Please guide me and direct me Lord that the words I write will be true and accurate and that they will bring glory to your name. Amen".

This writing has been one of the most extensive tasks I have ever put my hand to. I have been reminded day after day of God's Grace and the Love He has for me. I have re-visited places in my life that I had long forgotten or had buried deep in my memory not wanting to go there again. I have cried and wept over all but a few pages. Some of the tears have been of joy writing about the life I have that could only be possible in my relationship with Jesus. While others have been the uprooting of things in my life that have been covered up and callused in pain and the sorrow that I have had to endure, some of my own doing and others by the deeds of those that should have cared and loved me. And so now I present you with my life story: "Hell on Church Street"

Table of Contents

Chapter 1

The Top of the Stairs

It was very late at night or very early in the morning, I don't recall, as I heard the all too common yelling and screaming. I covered my head with a blanket to escape the threat of my being the cause of all the commotion and closed my eyes in fear. Then I heard my name being shouted. I jumped out of my bed, up off the closet floor where I slept, and ran as fast as I could to the sound of her voice as she was calling me. I asked myself as I hurried "What did I do? Am I going to be beat for something? I hoped not. Oh please, not a beating." I didn't know what to expect other than it wouldn't be good. It never was.

The house was ice cold and dark, the power had been turned off for many days now and there wasn't any coal in the bin for the furnace. Was this the reason why she was screaming for me, because the house was cold? It wouldn't be the first time I had to fill the coal bin in the middle of the night, hearing my dad yelling at me to get my lazy butt out of bed to the basement and fill the furnace. My feet were cold and I was running. Tears were rolling down my cheeks. I wiped them away and kept on going. One thing I knew was I had better hurry. I was trembling with fear, half asleep, and shivering from the cold. Then I saw her standing at the top of the stairs.

It wouldn't be the first time I would have been thrown down those stairs, getting a beating from the woman calling me, pounding me with her fist all the way down to the bottom, pulling my hair and screaming that she hated me. What would it be now? The buckle from a belt, an extension cord, the mop ringer, or would she scream at me and spit in my face? "What did I do," was the only thought going on in my mind as I got to where she was standing. She was in agony and crying, with tears rolling down her face. Something was terribly wrong. Being pregnant, she was close to her due date and in a great deal of pain, crying loudly, doubled over and pleading for me to help her. Here she was, this woman that has starved me, beat me, and kicked and hurt me so many times. She was always yelling and screaming, telling me how much she hated me, looking at me with eyes of hate, and now here she was begging for me to help her.

All of a sudden it came to me that now was the moment that I had dreamed of.

This is it and now is the time. I could end it here and now. No more beatings. No more being kicked in the ribs, punched in the face, or whipped with a hose. I wouldn't have to look at the pain on the faces of my brothers and sisters. No more hell. Jump her, smash her face into the wall, put her in a head-lock, and ride her down the steps, all seventeen of them, pounding her face in each step all the way to the bottom. Kill her. Yes, kill her now. This witch that has caused me so much pain, beat me so many times, and even tried to kill me more than once. Yes, here she is, this one that has denied me food to eat, choked me, and thrown piss in my face. Yes, end it now; kill her, who would ever know that I did it. *I hate you,* I thought, *and would rather you were dead.*

Then all of a sudden something moved over me, something like I had never experienced before; I felt sorry for her, standing there, in so much pain. She was crying so hard, pleading, and calling me to help her. I rushed to her side not realizing what I was doing. Putting my arm around her I helped her down the stairs where she would be safe. I got her to a chair and then I went out the front door running to get help. I ran as fast as I could to the square in the center of town looking for the police. I was so out of breath and yet I felt so new inside. My mind was clear and my thoughts were about saving a life and that of an unborn child. I had never felt like this before. I felt a newness. A sudden strength came upon me. Human lives were in the balance and it was up to me. I found a policeman and told him what was happening and where, and then I turned and started running back toward home as fast as I could. All the way I could hear the sirens and see the flashing lights.

When I got home the police had already arrived and the ambulance people had already left and were taking her to the hospital. I watched and listened as the police and others were talking about the appearance and smell of our house. I found myself being embarrassed at the condition of my home. There was no electricity for lights in the house. I remember following the beam of the flashlight with my eyes as someone pointed it, revealing the conditions we lived in.

Seeing what the light revealed was not a pretty sight. We lived on the last street on the edge of a small town. For some reason the city sewer would back up in to our basement. It would sometimes rise up to two feet or more. Everything on the floor would of course float to the top. There was weeks of laundry and garbage in standing sewer water in the basement. I recall the expressions on the faces of the police as they shined their flashlights down the basement stairs. I thought they might gag and throw up from the odor.

After a while the house was quiet as everyone had left. It had been hours now since I had run to town for help. I collapsed on a couch and fell asleep as the sun began peeking through the window for the beginning of a new day. As I woke up about an hour or so later, I could hear my brothers and sisters walking around, talking, wondering what was going on. We were all hungry because we hadn't eaten anything for days. What food we had was locked up in the cabinet. The groceries were under lock and key so we kids would not get into them. We were considered wasteful, ungrateful little &^#@%*. Everything in the freezer was spoiled and I could smell the rotten meat as I opened up the door to look inside. Everything in the refrigerator was spoiled too. I was so hungry that my stomach was hurting. My dad and Barbara wouldn't let us have food to eat. They said that we couldn't be trusted not to waste it. So we would have to eat under their supervision sitting at the table while they would eat in the living room. If we didn't drink the powered milk we would be forced to do so while our heads were held back and it was poured down our throats, gagging us and making us sick to our stomachs, throwing up.

Later that morning there were some people standing in the house, they identified themselves as from the state. They told us that they were there to help us until they could locate our father, and that we needed to leave with them now. The lady doing all the talking held a handkerchief over her mouth as she spoke. It didn't take long and we were all put in to cars and driven off. We were told not to take anything with us that they would get us anything we needed to take with us to our first foster home. I recall telling them that I wanted to wait for my dad to come home, but this was met with, "No, you have to leave with us now."

It would be some time before I would see my brothers and sisters again, and as we drove off I turned, looking back, wanting to forget about all the hell on Church Street.

Chapter 2

Mother the Early Years

My mother was raised in a home where work, hard work from sun up to sunset, was the standard way of life. At a very young age she was taught to keep house, clean, and bake. In the summer time mother also helped plant and maintain a large family garden. There was the sowing, weeding and carrying of water in pails from the well. The garden had to be free from weeds and she would pull and dig them out by hand.

This was the hard time after the great depression and during the Second World War. The family had to live on what was grown in the garden for the entire year. There was also the food canning and all the work that this involved. Not only did my mother can, but she chopped the wood, built the fire and kept it going hot enough to boil water for the pressure cooker. For a young girl, she was most accomplished in the kitchen, and was expected to have the evening meal ready for the men when they came to the house from the fields and farm work.

Mother would be up early in the morning. She was responsible for the laundry. This meant building a fire to boil water and then carrying it to the washtub to do the clothes. Everyday mother did the wash by hand. Using a scrub board and brush, a large bar of lye soap to clean the clothes and rinse them, she would ring them out and hang them on the clothesline. All the while she was keeping a fire going in the cook stove, making meals, and helping with the farm chores. My mother's life was hard and being the only girl meant much more responsibility. She killed and dressed chickens and milked the cow. When she needed to take a break she sat in front of the sewing machine making her own clothes, and keeping up with the other mending that was needed in the home. This was the life my mother lived as a young woman. It was about to take a big change, a whole new dimension.

In the summer of 1946 mother was a young girl of about fourteen. She had already lived a long life, and now things were about to get tougher for her. She was pregnant, unwed, and under age. I can, with a sad heart, imagine what she was going through. The emotion she must have been feeling, and the daunting task of having to share the news with her mother. Here she was a frail little girl, having never been away from home much, and now going to have to answer the tough questions. *How long have you known? Why didn't you tell me?* All the time feeling guilty for her situation. Now to have her mother's words cutting deep into her already crushed heart, and the hope of the future gone. Feeling the shame that was being directed at her, all the time knowing that she was the victim, a child herself. Now having to live with the shame that was being imposed on her by having to protect the identity of the child's father. With determination, the family had to keep the secret, the thing she couldn't share with outsiders. She was stuffing the guilt for not stopping what had happened to her, with the feeling of having to protect the family name and the identity of the one who had assaulted her. Yet all the while she was bearing the uncomfortable feelings she had sitting at the dinner table with her assailant.

Being pregnant didn't change mother's situation. Her chores had to be completed. She still had to do the cooking and the baking. The laundry was still her responsibility, scrubbing the family clothes, rinsing them and hanging them out to dry, all the time being made to feel dirty and cheap for what had happened to her. As my mother would work in the garden I can imagine how she would withdraw and escape to the thoughts of how her life would be, far a way from home. In her thoughts she would hope for things she never had, being able to run and play with the other girls, maybe going to a dance and enjoying the music. Thinking what life would be like with her baby. Would it be a boy or a girl? And as she would plan and dream about another life, she would think about the boy down the road.

Chapter 3

Who wet the bed

"Gun Smoke starring James Arness," were the words coming over the television. The next thing I heard was, "All of you kids get your *&^% down to bed."

There wasn't any warning, no hug, no one saying good night, it was "Get your%$#*& in bed, now!"

I remember appealing softly to stay up and watch my favorite TV show only to be met with a slap upside the head, and the words, "Get your %$#@ in bed now if you know what's good for you."

So down the steps to my bedroom I went, with tears rolling down my face, choking back the emotion as my stomach and chest would heave and then I would catch my breath, holding it in so as not to be heard crying. I didn't want to make dad mad, or hear him tell me to stop, or what the &%$ are you crying for, knock it off before I give you something to bawl about, so to bed I would go. I climbed up the ladder to the top bunk and got under the covers, laying awake looking out the window. I had no thoughts as I lay there, no plan for the next day; I simply laid there choking back the sound of my crying, wiping the tears from my eyes and blowing my nose on my sleeve as I fell off to sleep.

As I woke for the new day I knew that it would not be a good one. Laying there so afraid, my mind was numb and like in a vacuum. I could hear the coffee pot on the stove percolating and the sound of cups as they were set out on the counter. The coffee was boiling faster and faster as the aroma, mixed with the smell of cigarette smoke, made its way down to my room. Now it wouldn't be long until I would hear, "Let's go! Get your %$#@ out of bed."

The smell of urine hung heavy in the room. I was so glad that it wasn't coming from me and I would be able to proudly proclaim that I didn't wet the bed. Then as I moved to get out of bed I knew that I had wet the bed too. Again I heard the words, "Get your &^%$%^ out of bed, now!"

I saw the look on my brothers' and sister's faces as we looked at one another. I didn't realize it then, but it was a look we would all share many more times to come as we grew up together - the face of fear.

As we all looked at each other we knew what was about to come. We stood there trying not to look guilty. Smoothing out our pajamas so as not to look wet, we stood there huddled together, afraid to move, feeling hopeless. All of us were wanting to run away but there was no place to go. Looking for some way to be rescued, reaching into our minds for hope. Maybe I would be overlooked and the attention would be fixed on someone other than me. I was trembling inside, so afraid I would look scared and get hit in the face for being a baby. Then I heard him calling to us to get our ^&&^$# upstairs.

There we were, the four of us, headed up the stairs, elbowing one another to make the other go up before us, shoving and fixing our attention on the other. Pushing my way up and holding back at the same time. Then dad heard us saying, "Stop pushing!" "Quit it." "Chuckie hit me!" "No I didn't!" "Ouch, you hurt me."

Then we would hear, "Get up here! Which one of you pissed the bed? Chuckie, get your &&% over here! Stand still, Susanne. Get moving and stop that ^%$# crying before I give you something to cry about. John, what's your problem?"
"I don't know."

"What do you mean you don't know, stupid? Get over here. Kenneth, get in line. Stand here. Stop that *&%$ bawling."

There we were, the four of us in a row, ages seven to eighteen months old being forced to stand there, all the while trembling inside, pleading with myself, hoping my lip would not quiver, *don't whimper*. All the time in my mind knowing what was to come. Yet I had to control myself. *Don't look at dad*. Pleading with myself not to cry. *Don't let the tears come, don't move, keep my hands and arm at my side.* I could feel and sense the fear in the room. I knew what it was and it was heavy, yet all the while I was fighting to control the emotion. *Don't show it, numb out.* My entire mind was stuffing, putting my thoughts in check, standing there with no option, nowhere to run, no one to help and my mind goes still.

"Who wet the bed?" were the next words I heard, as my eyes were looking at the floor.

Then he said it again, "Who wet the *(&% bed. We are going to stand here all day if that is what it takes, now I want to know which one of you little *&^% *& *($%^*^ wet the bed? Chuckie did you wet the bed?"

I knew that I had, and knew what would become of me if I said yes, and so right down the line he walked asking the same question over and over as he had his belt firmly wrapped around one hand while softly hitting the other. *Why did he hate me so much?* Back and forth he would go and stop in front of me and ask again if I had wet the bed, and I said no. At this point he reached and felt my pajama pants and asked, "How did your pants get wet?"

I answered that I didn't know. Then all of a sudden he turned around and started hitting me with the belt, yelling. "This is for lying!" he said as he continued hitting me.

He continued to hit me with the belt saying "Don't you ever lie to me you *&^% *&^%$. Stop that bawling &^^$ you!" as I tried to cover my backside with my hands to protect myself.

He hit me more and more and I cried out "My hands, oh my hands!" only to hear, "Get them out of the way then."

He continued to beat me as he took hold of one of my arms and beat me some more.

"Shut up and stand still. Stop your bawling, *&^% you." He yelled as I fell to the floor in pain, getting hit some more. Then I was told to go to my room until I was finished bawling.

Even at seven years old I could see the pain in my mother's eyes and knew that she was a hurting and abused woman. I know that mother spoke to my father about the way he treated us. I could hear mother pleading with him from behind the closed bedroom door. There were times that my father would slap and push her around, throwing her across the kitchen. Mother often had black and blue eyes for weeks on end. I would hear her talking to her mother on the telephone, begging for her not to come to our house.

Even at my young age I wished there was something that I could do to help her. I was so numb with fear, that I lived in a continual state of survival from one moment to the next never knowing when I would be the target of my father's rage.

Chapter 4

Head Injury

I was watching television and playing when I heard someone yell out, "Bedtime. Everyone get your *& %$) downstairs to bed."

I ran to the bathroom before I went down to bed, with what had happened this morning still fresh in my mind. I was given another beating with the belt for wetting myself in the night. I tried to hurry and get finished so to get to bed without being slapped for taking too long.

Climbing up the ladder to the top bunk at day's end meant two things for me at eight years old, the fear of being hit was less likely to happen, and I could cover my head and somehow, in my mind, escape the world around me. I would lay there with the blanket pulled up over my head and wrap myself tight and feel secure from the threat of danger. As I was finishing up in the bathroom I heard someone yell, "You better wash your hands when you're through!"

As I left the bathroom and crossed the living room floor headed for the stair way, my dad asked if I had washed my hands and then told me, "You better not be lying to me if you know what's good for you. Now move, get out of my way. You'd make a better door than a window," as I paused in front of the television on my way down the stairs.

There were six steps that led down to the next level of the basement and when I reached the bottom, I all of a sudden felt a hand grab hold of the back of my neck as I was slammed into the wall. The force of the thrust crashed me through the wallboard, and then there was another blow as my head snapped back from the first blow. I was dizzy and light headed as yet another blow came as someone was beating my head into the wall, and with this next blow my head hit a wall stud and I felt numb. Then everything went black. There was ringing in my ears, as I was knocked out unconscious. I could remember landing on the floor, motionless and then nothing.

As I woke later in the night I was in my bed. My body was thrashing back and forth, my skin was cold and wet, my head hurt so terribly bad, pounding and throbbing. I was dizzy and my chest was heaving harder and harder. I couldn't breathe flopping around on the bunk bed. My throat was swollen and my tongue was in the back of my mouth. I couldn't breathe, I couldn't talk, and my mind was moving in circles, faster and faster. The flashes of light in my mind were out of control. I was making noises that I had never heard or made before. All the muscles in my body were stiff. I had no control over anything. I was experiencing helplessness in the dark, afraid and alone, trying to call out, but there was nothing, no sound. Then all of a sudden someone was shaking me, talking, yelling, asking me questions. "What is wrong?" there was the sound of worry in the voice.

Then I was alone again. Fear gripped me. Every muscle in my body was stiff and I was in pain. Then a hand was forcing my mouth open, fingers digging into my cheeks. I felt the cold metal of a spoon at the roof of my mouth, the curved side down now in the back of my throat, pressing down and yet pulling forward. I couldn't breathe. I was choking to death. Someone was lying on top of me, holding me down. Voices. I could hear people sounding with concern as I clamped my jaw tighter and tighter. Fingers prying open my mouth, feeling my teeth move across the spoon as someone was trying to pull my tongue forward.

Now there were more people in the room, I could hear my mother weeping as I was picked up and placed on a stretcher. They strapped me down, now even moving faster I was carried up the stairs, across the living room floor, out the door I was rolled. I was thrashing harder and harder. I couldn't control my movements. I was clamping down on the spoon that was in my mouth. I could see the flashing red lights as I was put into the back of the ambulance, I was being held down by someone as a strap was put around my head, my arms were tied down with bands, and then the doors were closed. I felt the vehicle moving forward as a needle pierced my arm. The siren was loud, and then nothing. For a moment I lay there, I was motionless, lying still, and then I was out.

When I woke up I could hear the sounds of people in the room. My eyes were heavy and closed. I attempted to open them, but drifted back to sleep again. I wasn't feeling any pain. However I was feeling the beating of my heart in my head. As my heart pounded I could feel pressure behind my eyes, as though they were too large to stay in the sockets. And once again I drifted off to sleep. I knew that my mother was with me there as I could smell her perfume and hear her voice as she asked, "Will he be okay?"

My entire body was aching with pain. I was so tired. What had happened to me I didn't seem to know, but what I was thinking about was my surroundings; the sounds coming from down the long hallway; the squeaking of wheelchairs and rolling carts hitting the wall. The smells were all new to me. Some of the scents were welcoming while others were not so nice - stale and musty.

I was sleeping again, dreaming; lights flashing in my mind; everything moving so fast. I was thrashing again, my neck was extremely stiff, and I was shaking and shivering from being so cold.

Later that day I was wide awake and my mother was beside me as the nurse took my blood pressure and checked the bags of fluids that were being added into my veins. My temperature was 104 degrees and I had been having grand mal seizures, dozens of them. They had lasted for over eight hours. I was now extremely cold. I was lying in a bed of ice. My fever was too high at 104 and the doctors were concerned that I had a suffered a brain injury. Then a doctor walked in to the room I could hear him talking to my mother, and then he turned and spoke to me.

"How are you doing? Are you okay?" he asked, not expecting an answer. "You took some fall, some fall down those stairs," he said. "You will have to stay here for maybe a few weeks because we need to take some more tests before we can send you home."

I was feeling emotionless, numb, and extremely void of feeling anything, except for the pounding of my heart in my head. I didn't realize it, I had no way of knowing, and no one was saying anything to me about it, however I was a very sick little boy, and the hope for my future was grim.

Chapter 5

The Doctor's Office and the Bus Ride

As the doctor gently ran his fingers through my hair, he would pause and gently press on my head, all the while making small talk with my mother. The office was a smaller room on the third floor of a large building in downtown St. Paul, Minnesota. I recalled how mother and I would walk from our house to the bus stop. This is where she caught the bus every morning for work. Now today I was with her. The office door opened and a nurse came in with a large folder and handed it to the doctor. He opened it and took the x-rays out and clipped them one at a time on to the light box to view them. As he was doing this mother and I sat on large wooden chairs, the kind that had a square piece of leather on the seat with round brass tacks holding it in place. My mother was looking sad as the doctor asked her to take a look at one of the pictures. He had a measuring device and was making notes on the film as he talked. Then he would come and stand next to me and with some kind of a large scissors looking thing he would measure my head, all the while making notes in a folder and talking to mother about what he saw.

The doctor felt that it would be in my best interest to be taken to some place in Rochester called the Mayo Clinic. As the doctor turned the light box off, he placed the film back into the folder and handed it to mother. I remember him saying something about my sleep and giving mother a prescription for some medication for me. Wishing me good luck he said that he would see me in a few weeks as we left his office. I loved being with my mother as we walked and stopped in front of the elevator.

The elevator was the kind that had a large lever to open the door with, and after the door was opened it had another door that folded to the side. This was fun for me as I got to close the doors by myself, with a warning not to get my figures pinched. Inside, mother let me push the big button with the number one on it, and turn the crank that closed the inside door. I would have loved to do this all day, however, with mother holding my hand, we left the building through the large revolving glass doors.

It was a busy afternoon in down town. The cars were stopping and going for the traffic lights, their horns blowing with the sounds of trucks and city buses. I could smell the gas and see the exhaust coming from the back of the buses and cars. I liked the smell. We walked a few blocks, stopping at the corners and waiting for the light to change so we could cross the busy street. Then we entered Steins pharmacy through the side door. I had been here before with mother and would like to sit at the fountain on the stools and make them go around, but not today mother said. Everyone greeted us as we walked in and sat down. My mother worked here and this is where she would take the bus every day. It seemed to me a long way from home, but I liked the ride. Today when mother ordered something for me to eat she walked to the back of the store to talk to her boss. I could see her there as he came out from behind the counter and stood there with her talking, he would look my way from time to time and once he smiled at me. As they finished the conversation my mother walked to where I was and visited with her friends as I ate my lunch. When I was finished with my meal we headed out the door for the walk to the bus stop. I liked riding the bus. It was up high and as I could look out the window I could see everything from up here.

There were many bus stops between where mother worked and the stop by our house, and I got to pull the cord for the buzzer for the other people's stops. My mother made this ride everyday at this time, so she was acquainted with the other passengers. I could tell as she was pleased to introduce me to people and would always smile when doing so. Today however my mother was troubled by something. She was really hurting inside, being concerned about my health and me, and yet I could see that there were other things haunting her too. She seemed so distant and withdrawn, caught up in a life drama that I'm sure was spinning out of control for her. I felt so bad for my mother as much as I knew how to do. I hurt for her so much. I had seen so many things going on in her life and now she was worrying about me too. I wished that she would not be hurt anymore and that I wouldn't have to see her cry.

We were soon to be at our stop as I had memorized all the stops on the route. I could tell whose stop was next and would watch as they got off the bus. I could see our stop in the distance as mother said, "Go ahead and pull the buzzer," as she was anticipating my next request before the words even came out of my mouth.

As we stopped, mother took my hand and said, "No jumping off the bus today." It was fun jumping from step to step and then to the ground, but I wouldn't be doing that today. So with mother holding my hand, she turned to wave as the bus pulled away.

As we walked up the street I saw my friends playing and riding their bikes. They would ride up to us and ask where we had been and if my mother had brought me anything. They wanted me to stay and play. As mother gently squeezed my hand I said, "No. I have to go home."

I didn't appeal as I knew mother by her mood and would have heard no a second time. So as we walked home my friends rode their bikes in circles around us having fun with their new skills of riding with no hands. I didn't know it then but I wouldn't be playing with them ever again.

Chapter 6

Rochester Trip

The sun wasn't even up. The lights were all on and people were talking. I could hear mother, dad and the new baby sitter, Barbara, talking. They were all at the kitchen table. I could hear mother giving instructions about the house, the kids and what to do about this and that. Barbara would be living with us and babysitting the other kids until I was well again, and while mother and I went on a trip. She was an eighteen year-old girl that was recommended by some friends of the family. As I made ready for the bathtub, mother showed me the new clothes I would wear on the long bus trip. After breakfast we would take the city bus down town to the Greyhound bus station.

After eating and washing up mother and I walked down the street to the bus stop. We had been there only a few moments when we stepped up into the bus for our ride down town. As we rode to town, mother made sure that I didn't go to sleep. I was tired and my head hurt, and yet mother made sure that I followed the doctor's orders. I was sure mother needed some sleep too, probably more than me, but she remained steadfast and gave me the best care she could.

Wow, I had never been to a bus depot before. There were several buses lined up under the large over hang that ran the total length of the depot. There were people carrying suitcases, some had shopping bags with handles on them, while others carried boxes that had been taped closed and tied with heavy string. The men working there had on matching uniforms and were loading suitcases in the area under the bus. I would have liked to have gotten a closer look and mother surely realizing this, directed my attention to the café' counter. I loved this! There was so much going on with the many people and the sounds of a busy place. As I was sipping my hot chocolate I could hear someone talking over the loud speaker, I looked around because I wanted to see who it was. This person was directing people to the bus, and as we finished our drinks, I listened as the man over the loud speaker said, "Rochester, Winona, Des Moines - gate two." Mother, with me in tow, headed for the gate. I was in no hurry as there was so much going on here and I didn't want to miss a thing. Looking back for a moment there was the man with the microphone standing where we had checked our bags, and I watched him as he said once more, "Des Moines and points south, final call, gate two."

The bus was a lot bigger than the city buses, and we sat up really high. Even though I had been awake for almost two days I was wide awake now. I watched as people climbed on the bus, we already had our seats, and I found the buttons on the side to put the back down. Some people were already asleep while others smoked cigarettes, and some sipped coffee. This was my first long bus trip and I was enjoying myself. Looking out the window I saw people on the street. I waved to them and it was great when someone waved back. I was having fun with this bus ride and now we were on our way to stay with my mother's aunt who lived in Rochester. Mother told that she was her mother's sister, and that made her my great aunt. I was so tired but mother said that I was under doctor's orders to not have any sleep until I had some test taken. Oh how I wished it was over already. When we pulled into the bus station at Rochester, mother said, "Look there's Aunty now!" as we saw her looking in our direction, waving and welcoming us.

After a short ride in the car we arrived at Aunty's home. Entering the front door I would have thought we were at grandmother's house. Everything was clean and fresh and smelled so very good. There was even something cooking in the oven and that fresh baked smell was in the air. As Aunty showed us the house, there on the kitchen counter was a fresh apple pie.

Chapter 7

The Mayo Clinic

As we arrived in radiology we were met by a nice lady in a nurse's uniform, holding a clipboard. She asked my name, looked at my new armband, and then had me sit in a wheel chair. This was exciting and I was already thinking about wheeling myself down the long hallway. The nurse and my mother had other plans, however, as they rolled me down the corridor to another waiting room. The waiting was what I didn't like. To nod off and go to sleep was what my body wanted to do. My head would fall forward as I began to doze off, only to wake up from the motion of going forward. My mother would engage me in conversation and every so often rub my arm with her hand. She was doing this when my name was called.

I was rolled in to a room that had a large window. Soon a lady came in and said that she was there to give me a haircut. So, placing an apron around my neck, she shaved off all of my hair. Then another woman started to wash my head with soap and water and as she was drying me off, someone else came in pushing a cart with all kinds of stuff on it. I wanted to look and see what was on the cart, but I was instructed to remain still. I was now having ointment from a small silver tube put on my head. It was cold, and I recall the lady apologized for that.

I was cold sitting in the recliner type chair and I was tired, but instructed not to fall asleep. Then they were attaching wires to my bald head and reminding me to sit still. The testing went on for a long time for me. I was constantly reminded not to fall asleep. Then the nurse came and said that I would like the next test. So, as she closed the door someone over a speaker asked me if I could hear them and I answered yes. Then they started a light test to measure my brain wave pattern. The lights of the room were turned off and I was instructed to close my eyes for a moment. "Now, Charles, open your eyes." they said.

And so checking the wire connections again, I was having one more test. This one used strobe lights. The light was flashing really fast and the people behind the glass were taking notes of what they saw. Finally, the nurse came in and said that I could go to sleep. This was going to be the last test for the day. It didn't take me long until I was out and fast asleep.

I was waking up as people were taking the wires off of my head. Then with warm soap and water they washed me up and mother and I were soon on the way to still another appointment, but not until mother took me out for lunch. I was embarrassed over the bald head. My mother, realizing this, wheeled me in to the gift shop and purchased me a baseball cap. The clinic had tunnels under the city that took you to different buildings. I was having fun for a small boy, but I could tell that my mother was tired and worried. I am most confident that not only was she concerned about me, but she must have been thinking about the other children at home and how they were getting along with the new babysitter, Barbara. She was only 18 years old and mother had not known her long before she came to stay with us.

Life was not easy for my mother nor had it ever been. I could tell as we were away from home that she would at times escape to a place in her thoughts. Where she would go or what she was thinking about, I had no way of knowing. However, even as a young boy I knew that her heart had been broken many times

Our home was not a peaceful place to live. Yes, there were times when the atmosphere was more pleasant than others. For example if we had people over for a birthday party for one of us kids, or when my grandparents would pick us up for church. My mother's parents went to a church that was not far from their house. We would go with them on Sunday mornings and afterwards they would take us out to lunch somewhere. My grandmother was always introducing us to people and they would always ask if I was one of Audrey's children. There was sadness that would come over my grandmother's face when she would talk about my mother. My mother's parents never seemed to like being at our house. I knew even at eight years old that they didn't like my father. No one ever said anything negative about him to me, but I could sense it. I wonder if they knew the way my dad hit mother when he was mad, or the way he treated me and my brother and sisters.

As we sat in the clinic waiting for my last appointment for the day, it was comforting knowing that my mother was there with me. Mother was sad today however, and she seemed to be more withdrawn than usual. I was hoping that it wasn't over me, though I'm sure some of it was. I noticed that she would wipe a tear from her eyes every so often. When I would ask her if she was alright she would say to me, "Now don't you worry about me Honey."

The doctor walked in to the room where we had been waiting. With a folder in his hand one doctor started to share with mother their findings. He told mother that I had suffered an injury to my brain from blunt force trauma to the head. He said that I had some scar tissue on my brain and that they would like to remove. This would require surgery that could have possible lasting effects on me. As we left the office that day my mother was in tears and sad as she seemed to drift away in her thoughts. I would have liked to do something about her pain but what could I do? I was only eight and it seemed the more I was concerned about mother the more she showed concern for me. So we took a taxi to Mother's aunt's house to spend one more night before the bus trip home.

Things at home seemed different somehow but I wasn't sure how. It didn't feel the way it did before I went on the bus trip. My father didn't seem to be any kinder to mother and he was continuing to yell and get angry over the smallest things. The babysitter was still living with us. It seemed that she moved in while we were gone and I remember there being an argument between my parents over the matter. One night my father, after being mean to my mother, walked out the door and as he left the house slammed the door and didn't come home until the next morning. This kind of thing went on for some time. Then late one night I woke up to some yelling and the sound of someone crying. I went up the stairs and saw a man sitting at our kitchen table bleeding and looking really beat up. My father was giving him wet towels to wash his face with and when he saw me told to get my rear end back to bed. As I laid there awake I was scared and felt concern for my mother as well. There never used to be so many people coming and going from our house. In some ways I welcomed all the people because we were not being treated so badly, but in other ways even at eight years old I knew that my mother didn't approve of all the people that Barbara was bringing to our home with her at all hours of the night. Her friends smelled like booze and were loud and made a lot of noise waking up everyone in the house and now even her brother had moved into our house.

Chapter 8

Mother is Killed

The sun wasn't even up when Barbara and her brother Walter got to the house. It was not even five a.m. yet. They had been out all night long with their friends drinking and partying. A few moments after their arrival, there was a loud knock at the door. It was three of their friends. I could hear them talking and laughing, and the smell of their booze and cigarettes made its way down to my bedroom. Seems that they wanted to party some more, and had brought their fun to our house. I had been awakened by the noise and so I could hear them in the kitchen, laughing and talking loudly. Then I heard my mother, as they awakened her also. She was now in the kitchen preparing to make them some coffee and breakfast. I heard her ask them to keep the noise down as not to wake the children. My dad was going hunting early this morning and I was surprised that I didn't hear him up, getting ready to go.

There sitting on the counter top beside the kitchen sink was my dad's hunting gear. He had put everything out the night before with plans of leaving very early in the morning. He had his hunting rifle out and his pistol, along with the rest of his gear. As the coffee was brewing on the stove, Vernon, one of Barbara's friends, picked up the rifle and was looking at it. He held it up and was looking down the barrel through the site. This was an absolute no-no. No one at our house ever touched one of dad's guns. Everyone else knew to never touch one of my dad's guns as well. That is why he left them out. No one dare to touch them. After looking at the rifle Vernon put it down and picked up the pistol and examined it. Then he pointed it at my mother in reckless fun as she placed her hand over her heart in disbelief. He then quipped, "I gotcha" as he pulled the trigger and the gun went off. A bullet passed through my mother's hand,

Striking her in the heart, he mortally wounded her. The police were called and when they arrived at our house, they picked my mother up and immediately rushed her by a squad car to Ancker hospital in down town St. Paul. The surgeons worked for five hours in an attempt to save her life. Unable to repair her wound, my mother died at eleven-thirty that morning, Saturday, November 11, 1961.

Monday afternoon I was seated on a pew in the second row at the church where my mother's parents attended. My sisters, brothers and I were all dressed with new clothes and as I looked around I could see some people I knew, but a lot of them I didn't recall ever seeing before. My mother's parents were sitting across from where we were and beside us were my father's mom and dad and his family. Every so often mother's mom would bring someone over to see us kids and they would hug us or give us kisses. They all looked so hurt and sad that my mother was gone. There were people walking past the casket, stopping for a minute and then moving on. Some were crying while others shook their heads in disbelief. I wanted to know what was going on, so I got up from where I was sitting and before my dad could grab my hand, I was standing and looking down at my mother laying there. She looked so peaceful and pretty, wearing her glasses and lips, red with lipstick. I knew inside that this would be the last time I would ever see her and I was crying and hurting so badly that my mind was numb and my heart was full of fear of what would become of me. Then Grandmother came over and stood with me. Taking my hand she reassured me that someday, I would see my mother again in a place called heaven. That afternoon we drove to the cemetery and laid my mother to rest.

On Tuesday afternoon, the day after mother's funeral, my father stood in a courtroom beside the man that had killed her waving a bible in his hand and pleaded with the judge not to charge him with any crime. Vernon Drake would be set free. He was never to be charged with any crime or spend a day in jail.

Chapter 9

The Road to Church Street

We had spent the whole day loading the U-haul truck. Now we were driving south headed to our new home in a place called Georgetown. The cab of the truck was crowded with four of us kids, two dogs, a cat, and my father and Barbara.

John, my brother had been hit by a car crossing the street a few weeks earlier and so he would be staying with our mother's parents until his cast was off. Then he would be joining the rest of us at our new home in Illinois. The cab of the truck was hot and it stunk with the smell of the cats mixed with Barbara's body order. I was sure she never took a bath because she always smelled this way and today was no different. Sometimes I would have to take a breath and hold it as long as I could and then exhale into the sleeve of my jacket and then draw another one so as not to have to inhale the order.

The trip to Georgetown was a long way from anything I had ever known and this is where we really started to experience the hatred of Barbara. She would pull my sister's hair or dig her fingernails into my brother's arms. I would from time to time get an elbow in the ribs and my little sister would get kicked in the back while trying to get comfortable lying on the truck floor.

Then when she would cry out from the pain Barbara would say, "Oh I'm sorry hon." and pretend that she did nothing intentional. The look on her face was the face of hate and it really started to show on this drive south. It would continue to get worse for the remainder of the drive, and for years to come. Her eyes were dark and set deep in her face and she seemed to pierce right through us with her stare, the faces she made toward us showed more of her hate. I was really missing my mother and it seemed like forever ago that I saw her lying in the casket at the church.

Somewhere about half way to Illinois my dad threw the cat out of the truck window because it had urinated on the floor and the place was stinking really badly. My little sister wanted to get up from the floor because she was all wet because of the cat, but my dad told her to keep her ^%$# on the floor until we stopped somewhere to get something to eat. I recall feeling so bad for her even then as she was only two years old at the time and was being treated so badly.

When we finally did stop my father filled the truck up with gas while Barbara went in to the station to get us something to eat. When she came back to the truck she made us peanut butter sandwiches to eat and slammed them at us and then she told us not expect anything else until we got to our destination. As we were getting under way again I was elbowed again real hard in the ribs and Barbara took a hold of my face and twisted it in her hand. When my dad heard me moan he stopped the truck real fast on the side of the road and looking at me, told me to stop my *&^% complaining or I would get something to complain about, "Do you understand me you son (*^%$#?"

Then before we took off again my father threw the two dogs out of the truck and said, "Good luck boys." Then he started driving again.

Ever since mother was killed I had begun to internalize and stuff my feelings and hold the emotion back for fear of being hit or beat with the belt. If I asked a question or said anything, my father would reach across the cab and bust me upside the head. I would wipe my tears on my shirtsleeve and hold my mouth in my arm so not to let dad hear me cry. My mind would seem to become a vacuum and I would not even be aware of what was going on around me as I withdrew. Sometimes this would go on for hours or until my father would yell at me for not paying attention or yell at me for being stupid.

It was sometime around noon the next day when we finally pulled up to our new home on South Church Street in Southern Illinois. This is where I would spend the next several years of my life, and I wondered then if my mother could see me. I thought sometimes that I could see her walking past our house. I would wake up in the night at times and she would be there beside me.

I missed her so much and longed for the comfort that I would find only in her arms. It would be many years now before I would have the comfort of anyone holding me, loving me or saying that they loved me. I had begun a new life now that I would someday call "Hell on Church Street."

Chapter 10

My Report Card

Laying here in my bed I listened closely to the sounds of the house and didn't hear Barbara up yet. It was a school day and I planned to get out of the house before she even knew I was gone. I really didn't want to go to school today because it was report card day, but staying home would mean a beating for something. Last night's supper was more of her goulash and I am sure she had pissed in it. It wouldn't be the first time and I was told that I would have to finish what I didn't eat at the table for breakfast. So I went quickly and quietly looking at my brothers' and sister's faces as we could all communicate with our eyes. The unspoken question was in everyone's eyes, "Was Barbara out of bed yet?" Maybe she had taken a lot of her pills last night and would sleep all day. I was careful not to make any noise, as were the others.

My pants were damp but dry enough to put on as they had hung across the radiator all night to dry. This was the only way I had to dry my clothes. I had washed them the night before with ivory hand soap and rung them out the best I could before placing them over the radiator hoping that they wouldn't be too wrinkled to wear to school this morning.

I was dressed and starting out the front door when I heard the cussing and swearing at my sister from Barb telling her she was going to be late for school. Furthermore, she was screaming wanting to know where I was and then she slapped my sister in the face telling her that she would have to eat breakfast before she left.

"I wouldn't want you telling anyone that you didn't eat at home," she yelled.

This was all an attempt to cause my sister to be tardy, so when she got home from school there would be an excuse to beat her for being late. I could still hear her screaming and swearing as I walked down the street.

This day in class would be no different than any other for me except that it was report card day. As I sat at my desk, I was so far away and deep in my thoughts hoping that I didn't get an *F* in anything as I would be big trouble tonight at home for my being stupid. The last time I got an *F* on my report card it was in Spelling. Dad made me sit at the kitchen table for hours until I could spell every word correctly. He would come into the kitchen and say, "Okay, spell this word." If I got it wrong he would hit me in the back of the head and call me by my nickname *Stupid little son*%$@$*. I would try to memorize the words, but was never any good at it and the more I misspelled, the dumber I was, and the more I would get hit in the back of the head. Finally, dad told tell me to get my stupid %$# to bed before he really got mad. And *Stop that *#^&* bawling before I give you something to cry about, you *&^$^ baby.*

I could never understand what was going on in the classroom, not that I didn't try. I did but I just didn't get it. My mind was blank and I stared at the blackboard and numbed out. I couldn't stay focused, and paid very little attention to my teacher. I lived every moment of my day in fear of what would happen when I would get home. If Barbara would have seen me this morning I would have had to eaten last night's supper, or corn flakes with powdered milk, for breakfast. This stuff made me sick. It was never mixed well, always warm and the lumps floated to the top of the glass. Not eating wasn't an option. If I resisted and didn't eat it in Barbara's time frame, I was considered an ungrateful little *&@#$ and would have it poured down my throat while she dug her finger into my cheeks to force my mouth open. But now I was at school, and for a few hours I was safe.

As lunchtime approached I had a decision to make; go home for lunch and get a beating for something or stay here and clean tables for a free lunch. I chose to stay. I saw my sister in the hallway and we always asked the question *is Barbara in a good mood*? We knew that the mood could change in an instant and we could be subject to a beating. She hated us and had threatened to kill us all more than once.

As I sat there at my desk I thought about what had happened to my little sister a few days ago. She was beat with a belt, picked up by her hair and thrown across the floor. The welts on her body, her four year-old body, swelled up and were red and blue with color. Barbara filled the bath tub up with water and ice cubes and put my little sister in it to soak in order for the swelling to go down. She was yelling at her for not keeping her hands and arms out of the way while she was being beat, and to stop crying before she got her face smashed. I felt so hopeless, not being able to help her. I sat here at my desk thinking about this and dreaming about killing Barbara for what she did to my sister. I would dream of how I would do it, how I would make her suffer. I hated her and it was a feeling deep inside of me. I wanted her dead more than anything in my life. I would think about it so much that the rage would build up inside of me until my head would hurt.

Walking home, I was cold as the wind and snow blew hard against my face. I would turn and walk backwards to protect my face from being frost bitten. I wondered if maybe my dad would be home today, if maybe he would deal with Barbara as he had on a few occasions, taking her upstairs and bending her over his knee and whipping her with the belt. Us kids would be standing downstairs listening as he hit her with the belt. We never said a word as we looked at each other about this, but I was celebrating the moment inside, while at the same time knowing that it would be taken out on one of us kids later on. I hoped Dad would be home. Barb didn't beat us when he was there. *Where was he,* I would wonder, not sure if I ever did get the answer to the questions I asked myself.

As I got closer to home I could see that dad's truck wasn't there. So, I stood outside the house next to the fireplace chimney holding my report card in my hand fearing what would happen to me when dad got home, yet wanting to hear the sound of him coming down the street towards home so I could go into the house out of the cold.

Chapter 11

Going to Work with Dad

Sitting in the front seat of the company truck riding down the highway with the window down was a fun time. The wind was blowing in my face and through my hair as I had my head out the window. It made my head itch, and I loved it. Summertime was here and I got to go to work with my dad. These days were the only good times I ever recall spending with my father.

As I looked out the window I could count the telephone poles as we drove by. I had to count fast though because, as my dad confessed himself, he drove fast. I mean he seemed to drive faster than anyone else and the other drivers were slow pokes. In fact, all the other drivers had names and my dad knew them all. For example there was "Stupid." This guy, according to dad's explanation, "If he had a brain he would be dangerous," and probably paid someone off to get his driver license. Then there was your "mother too". This is the guy that dad would glare at while passing him doing ninety, swearing and wearing his meanest, ugly look. If the guy said something in response that dad didn't like, he turned and swerved toward him to scare the bejeebies out of him. Yes, this was a day at work with dad and we were going to our next stop.

My father was a water systems installation man. The salesmen from the office had already been to the customer's house and sold them a water softener. Dad's job was to go and hook them up. I had my role in the process as well, and I was always introduced to the customer by dad. He would tell them that I was his oldest and I was there to help put in their new water softener. So, as the homeowner showed us where they wanted the unit installed, dad would tell me what he needed and I would go to the truck and get it. There was a list of things I knew we always needed for the job. I would start with the torch, striker, pipe wrenches, fittings, and other stuff. Then I stood by watching my dad work. I got so I could anticipate what dad would need and have it in my hand ready to hand it to him. When it was time for the actual water tank, I would go out to the truck and carry it in to the house while my dad finished up the plumbing. Once this was finished, I would go and start bringing in the salt bags. Salt was used for the regeneration process in the water softener. The bags weighted fifty pounds and I really felt strong knowing that I could carry them.

As we finished up the job I would gather all the tools and other equipment and take them out to the truck. The last thing I did was to gather up all the empty salt sacks and throw them in to the back of the truck. Sometimes, as I carried out the empty salt sacks, they were not empty. It seemed that dad used me as the bagman as he was stealing from the customers.

Somehow inside I would feel uncomfortable about this as we were riding in the truck. I was aware that dad could tell that I knew something wasn't right, but we never did talk about it. As the years went on this kind of activity would continue, and as I grew I learned how to read my dad's behavior like a book. It was easy to know if he was up no good or had gotten away with something. It was all over his face.

Riding in the truck with dad on those warm summer days were some of my favorite times growing up. It was when I could feel something toward him other than fear. We would drive the back roads of southern Illinois all summer long installing water softeners and iron filters. Home was so far away. I didn't even think about it until we stopped to fill the truck up with gas. Yes, it was about time to head home. Somehow inside I would go numb as I looked out over the fields getting closer to the only life I knew. I hated it but there was nothing I could do about it. I wouldn't dare speak about it to dad, not even on one of his best days. No way. I tried once and he turned and looked at me with a guilty stare and said nothing.

As we pulled into the driveway at home it was already dark and dad told me to take all the salt sacks out of the truck and put them in the shed. Then he told me when I was finished with that, he wanted me to be sure to fill two five gallons gas cans with some of that new fresh gas we had put in the truck. This was something that I did for dad every Friday night. I liked the smell of gas and I could siphon it now without getting any in my mouth. Dad told me once that I was getting pretty good at it and to keep up the good job.

Chapter 12

Pop Bottle Shopping

Today was Friday and I had plans to go to the river after school and do some fishing and hunting for some crayfish to cook up. They were tasty cooked in butter over an open fire. My dad worked the late shift for the city water works department at the dam, and on the weekends all summer long this was where I lived. My brothers and I would set up camp on the river up from the dam about a quarter mile, and if dad wanted us he would walk out on the catwalk and call us. No matter how far we were up the river, we could hear the call, and we would head back. These were some exciting and peaceful times for me and I was free to be a boy of twelve. All I could think about all day while at school was the camping trip.

If I didn't let Barbara see me there would be no beatings when I got home. If she did see me there was no telling what would happen. One day I would kill her and bury the body where no one would ever find her and let her rot. I would shake my head to try and get rid of the thought of her and what I thought about doing but some days that is all I wanted to think about. As soon as I got home my brothers and I started getting ready to go. I gathered my cane pole and fishing stuff along with the new reel I ripped off from the hardware store the day before. I was glad that I didn't get caught doing that one. I liked it so I got it. After a while I would show it to my father and say that I found it at the river. So now I headed to the basement to get some night crawlers. Our father raised worms in large tubs for the purpose of selling them at the river, so we had all the fish bait we needed. Problem was, if dad found out I would get my head knocked off. We were always gathering up stuff and hiding it away for the river - things like rope, matches, blankets, and old canvas tarps. Almost anything could be used at the campsite in the imagination of a twelve year-old boy. My brother and I had been getting food ready all week and hiding it so Barbara wouldn't find it, but we still needed a few things. So we gathered up some pop bottles and headed for the store. We had figured out how to go shopping with pop bottles. At the local store, pop bottles were redeemed for a nickel and the quart size brought a quarter. So, with a few twelve packs under our arms, we were on our way to go shopping. We loved redeeming bottles and we were very creative in doing so. There were times when the money from our enterprise was all we had to eat with.

When you walked in to the store there was a large wooden bin for bottles. You would show them to the cashier, put them in the bin and redeem the cash. I had been doing this for years. Barbara and dad were big Pepsi drinkers and would go through three or four twelve packs in a weekend. The pop bottles would pile up until Barbara needed cigarettes or something then she would tell me to take the bottles to the store and get her some smokes. Like I said, I had been doing this for years and it didn't take me long to realize that the hand is quicker than the eye. Into the store I would go, bottles in each hand and under one arm. I put them in the bin and I was sure to make enough noise so that the cashier would hear me, turn to look and I would say, "Six twelve packs," when really I had deposited three. That was one hundred percent profit. Three dollars and thirty-six cents would buy enough food for a week at the river. We loved fresh fried fish and bread and butter to eat. It was better than anything we had at home.

With everything in my father's truck, and with my dog, Trooper, lying under my feet on the floor, we were on the way.

I loved my dog. He was given to me as a puppy by my auntie, and he would go anywhere I went. On many days he would be waiting for me after school and walk home with me. While we were camping he would always warn me if anyone was in the woods and he would growl when if anyone walked past our campsite or drifted by on the river in a boat. My dog was the best friend I ever had. I loved him and he loved me too.

We were so happy that we were finally here, and starting to set up the campsite. I got the fire going and then threw my line into the water. It wouldn't be too long and I would be catching some sunfish. With some bread and butter from the store, we were set for a great weekend of eating fish sandwiches.

Our camping adventures were an escape for me and I would try not to think about home and all that went on there while I was at the river. It was hard to erase the thoughts of what my sisters were probably going through and what Barbara was doing to them... the sight of her pulling their hair as she had it wrapped in her fist and slamming them into the wall with a look of hate on her face as she screamed. I wondered if they were being beat and choked or maybe being forced to stand in a corner all night long, or having piss put into their food.

I could live here the rest of my life and be happy. I would lay awake at night looking up at the stars, enjoying the peace and safety, dreaming about how things would be when I was far away from here. I dreamed of a nice home where there would be peace and no threats of harm, no beatings, a home free from violence, and I would see to it. There would be no more cussing and swearing. No one would ever hurt anyone. As I laid there I would envision what my life would someday be, and I would cry wishing that I could run away. Wiping the tears from my eyes I crawled into the tent with Trooper and fell off to sleep.

Chapter 13

Grandma and Grandpa

Things were moving at a fast pace today and no one was being beaten or slapped around. Barbara was running around with nothing on except her tee shirt and without her teeth in her mouth. Oh, how I hated her. She never took a bath and she always stunk of B.O., bad. All the windows in the house were open, the radio was playing, "One, Two, Three Red Light," and we were cleaning house. School was out for the summer and my dad's parents were coming to live with us. Cleaning house was some under taking. Everything was pushed in one direction toward the back of the house to the basement door. Then, with brooms, everything was swept down the stairs. The basement was a pit full of everything you could imagine. The washing machine was the ringer type that meant that you had to empty it of water when the wash was finished and then run the clothes through a ringer. When they were all rung out you rinsed them and started the process over again. This would continue all through the night. We had company coming. The laundry was sorted into piles. We had a pile of whites, colors, rugs and the "throw away." The "throw away" were the clothes and bed linen that had rotted from being there so long.

Everything went to the basement - bags of trash, cans, anything that you wanted to get rid of went down the stairs. Out of sight, out of mind. This was the *get ready for the good showing* time - the *everything is normal* time. The walls were washed with a rag, buckets of hot water, and soap by us kids. If the water was too hot for our hands, we were a little lazy &^$* and were open to having our face smashed. We worked all day and through the night without sleep on our hands and knees scrubbing floors and the walls. Oh, and the bleach… everything smelled like bleach.

Cleaning the kitchen cabinets was a real task. It could take two days alone. Dad would make us remove everything and stack the dishes in one area and the pots and pans in another. As we cleaned the cabinets if my dad found one streak we would get slapped upside the head. I always wondered how my dad could move so fast across the house to hit one of us kids. While we were cleaning dad would take his baked chicken out of the oven and in to the living room to eat while we worked. The smell of the food made me wish I could eat. I hadn't eaten all day long.

Once the cabinets were clean and approved it would be time to wash the dishes. Every dish in the house had to be washed, rinsed and dried and put on the counter top for inspection. Dad would pick the dishes up one at a time looking for some imperfection. If dad found one thing he didn't like we were slapped and had to start over again, and wash every dish in the house over. So there we were lined up at the kitchen counter... four kids... tired, scared, and washing dishes all night long. They looked at one another, taking our pain and hatred out on each other.

The next morning we had to finish anything that didn't get done the night before and be on watch for the arrival of my grandparents. I would think of how life was going to change once they got here. There would be no more yelling and beatings or getting punched in the face. I would be happy. For once in my life, I wouldn't have to be afraid any more. Oh, how I wished that they would get here soon. There was still time to get pounded or whipped with the belt. Then looking out the window I watched as my grandparents pulled into the driveway. Boy was I happy! All my fear had melted away. We had never been hit, slapped or worse, been beat, when we had company, and now people were here to live with us.

The next morning I woke up to the smell of pancakes. My grandpa was up early in the kitchen. The house sure smelled good! I couldn't recall the last time someone had made breakfast for us kids. Grandpa was whistling and singing a tune. The smile on his face was warm, and I could tell that he was happy to be here. Soon the other kids would join us in the kitchen for what seemed like a dream. There were so many pancakes and lots of stuff to put on them. We had honey, maple syrup, and homemade jam. Grandma had brought it with her for us. We had chocolate milk and orange juice and the house was filled with joy. It had been too long to remember the last time that I felt like this. We had real milk to drink, not the warm powered stuff with dry lumps in it.

Then all of a sudden Barbara walked in the room while grandpa was in the kitchen and gave us all her look of hate, with eyes that said they would rather beat us than look at us. So without even saying a word she had taken our joy away and told us to stop eating like pigs. She went on to say that our grandpa had better things to do than to spend his day cooking for us ungrateful little @#*&^%. Without missing a beat she was in the kitchen speaking as kindly as she could to Grandpa, as though nothing had taken place.

My grandpa was an interesting man who had raised his family during the Great Depression. He could make toys out of about anything. With an empty oatmeal box and some rubber bands he made a toy that once you rolled it on the floor, it would stop and roll back to you. He was handy this way, and with a piece of wood and his pocketknife he could whittle out a whistle that you could blow. We all wanted one.

One day, grandpa took an old tire and with his knife fashioned it into a swing. So with some rope we climbed up that big oak tree. Out on the largest limb we tied it off and the swing was complete. We had years of fun swinging on that old tire.

My dad's mother was a real champ. I liked my grandma and we got along well together. I liked the way she said my name. No one could ever say it like she could. She was special to me and I know that the feeling was the same with her. On many afternoons I would sit with her and watch her favorite television programs. Every day at the same time she did the same thing. After fixing us kids' lunch and being so nice, she would send the others to take a nap and the two of us would spend the afternoon together. I would sit on the arm of Grandma's big chair while she watched her shows and ate her lunch of grapefruit and cottage cheese. How she never got tired of eating the same thing every day was beyond me. Now and then she would have some fresh cheese with rye crackers. I even learned to enjoy them myself after awhile.

My grandma always treated me special. I never knew why and it wasn't something I thought up myself, but the love she shared with me was always warm and caring. Grandma would want to know what I thought about things, and so we talked about everything together. Sitting on the armchair I would share my thoughts and my dreams. We talked about the wife I would have someday and of how special she would be. She was a good listener and she would ask me questions about the things I shared with her. Grandma had a way of resting her elbow on the arm of the chair and raising her forearm and then letting it fall down again if she heard something she liked. This was one of those mannerisms a person has that is unique to only them, kind of like the way she said my name. Grandma would talk with me for what seemed like hours on those days. I would hold those times close to my heart and always remember the peace I experienced there on the warm summer days.

Chapter 14

Right Before My Eyes

As I walked up the sidewalk coming home from school I could hear the yelling and fighting. It sounded like Grandpa and Grandma. I ran around the house and came in the back door as I heard grandma yelling, "Who are you? God!"

Then as I got closer I saw dishes flying toward grandpa. He ducked one and was hit with another in the back of the head. "Please stop!" He was pleading with her not to throw her good dishes at him.

I turned around and went back outside and stood by the fireplace chimney. I was lost in emotion. My thoughts were numb and like in a vacuum. My feelings were hurt and I couldn't understand how this could be going on now after things were so good.

"I hate you ^%$#@!" Grandma would say.

"Please stop this!" Grandpa was pleading.

I didn't know what to do. I was clenching my teeth harder and harder. Squeezing my eyes closed tightly. Wanting to escape the drama I was now experiencing. Then I heard the china cabinet crash to the floor and saw Grandpa came running out the back door headed to the shed with two cups flying by, missing his head. I ducked around the side of the house and had a good view of Grandpa in the shed. He was weeping, with his hands up in the air, turning in circles. I felt so bad for him and didn't want him to know that I was watching. I was seeing something that I wished I had never saw that day. My heart was broken. Things didn't ever seem the same after that day. I had, for a few months, lived in a house without violence, yelling, and screaming. Now my peace all seemed to crumble right before my eyes.

This was not something new for my grandparents. They had behaved like this for many years. Even while their own children were at home there was violence and abuse of different kinds in the home. They could be heard screaming and fighting by the neighbors half a mile down the road. The girls of the home had the abuse at the hands of their father, and my dad had as well. The sickness of sexual abuse at the hand of Grandpa even made its way into our home and my sister was but one more victim of the inappropriateness. The yelling and screaming was a way of life back then, and now here it is now continuing in our house. I ran to the shed where I had a fort and climbed up the ladder and laid there with my head pounding with pain. I cried and cried so much for myself and for my grandpa too. I had never seen them fight or ever heard the words they were saying. Mean, cutting words meant to hurt and inflict harm.

The next morning I was up early and headed to the woods with my dog Trooper. I didn't want to see anyone and was too embarrassed to even look at Grandpa and really didn't know what to make of Grandma either. I didn't quite understand why he let Grandma treat him that way or why she was so mean. My thoughts for both of them changed that day. It was sad but I couldn't seem to help it. They had hurt my feelings. I had been let down by those that I had so much faith in, and I doubted if they even knew it. Here in the woods I had a place of safety from my home and family. I had a place that no one even knew about. So I lay down and cried some more and then I fell off to sleep wondering what would ever become of me.

Chapter 15

The 2 x 2 Beating

The final bell rang and school was out for the day, and for a fifth grader that was great. My walk home always took me past my stomping grounds in the woods. We lived on the corner of Church and Division Street. Division was the last street in the city limits and so across the street from our house was the country. Our neighbor had a farm there and we kids played back in the woods and sometimes we would spend the day picking up black walnuts with grandfather when he lived with us. There was also a river there that passed through the woods. If we went one way it took us back toward the school and in the other direction it took us to the camp spot we had up from the dam. We walked this way home from school every day. Sometimes we would jump on the back of one of the neighbor's horses and ride bare back and take the long way home.

Today as I walked I was coming up the hill from the gully with a fresh picked pear in each hand. I was about to cross the street when my sister ran past me yelling and screaming, headed toward the house. I could hear her yelling and carrying on for blocks and I was sure everyone in the neighborhood could too. It seemed a little odd that she was headed home like this, but I was accustomed to hearing this and didn't give it a second thought.

As I approached the yard to the house the yelling and screaming had added yet another voice, Barbara. She sounded as angry as I had ever heard her sound. As I walked up the steps to the porch I could see that she was in another one of her rages, with the look of hate deep in her eyes. It was written all over her face and she had her attention focused on me. She ordered me into the house and as soon as I entered I was met with a fist to the face as she proceeded to kick and punch me. She was screaming at me yelling, "Why did you hit Susanne?" all the while pounding me with her fist as spit was coming from her mouth.

Then she ordered Susanne to go get a stick.

She was in a violent rage and kept screaming at me, "You're going to get it you little&*(^%$."

I was crying and pleading, asking what it was that I had done, saying, "I didn't do anything." All the while being beat, kicked and punched.

"I'm going to kill you!" She screamed, "You son of a #%$#@" as she hit me in the face yet again and again. With a low deep hate-filled voice she yelled at me, the glare of hate in her eyes and the look on her face.

She hit me with another blow and knocked me to the floor as my sister arrived with a two by two picket off of the falling down front porch. As I tried to get up from the floor I was met with a blow to the ribs, then another. I fell back trying to defend myself with my arms over my head. She kept hitting me, blow after blow, pounding my arms as I tried to protect myself. I heard the thump of the picket hitting my body. I rolled into a ball, arms over my head, to protect my face, all the time being beat on the arms, kicked and called a liar.

"You lying little &^%$#!" and I was being kicked some more in the back. She was in yet a more violent rage and spit was still coming from her mouth as she yelled.

This went on for what seemed like hours. I wasn't feeling pain anymore, only the blows from the 2x2 hitting me in the back. My mind went numb and somehow, finally, I was able to get up and run to get away outside. Then I felt another blow as I rolled down the porch steps and then another blow as she threw the board at me and hit me in the back. I ran as fast as I could, falling and getting up. Somehow I ended up across the street on the neighbor's front steps. As I fell hitting their front door I was out cold.

The next thing I remembered was sitting on the couch in the neighbor's living room being held by the lady there. It was clear that I could have been killed and how I escaped, I wasn't sure.

Now I was begging the neighbor lady, "Please don't send me home." as she was putting ice on my face and washing my back with a cloth.

I felt like my ribs were broken and the welts on my back were beginning to swell and burn with pain. I was here for what seemed like hours when I heard the unmistakable and familiar sound of my dad's 1959 Mercury coming in the distance. For so long that was the sound of help coming. Safety was on the way. When dad was home we didn't get the beatings from her hand, but his presence didn't stop the other forms of abuse and I wasn't feeling any safety tonight. I was sure I would get the belt from him as well because my sister had said I had hit her.

There were always countless accusations against us kids by Barbara, and any denial of the indictment would be met with the belt or the chewing of a bar of soap for lying. I recall my dad asking me once why Barbara would lie. If I was so bold to say something it would be met with denial. So I stood there as she looked on. If you spit out the soap, you would have to swallow it. Somehow this was suppose to be good for me as I can recall dad telling me that this was for my own good.

I was sure that it wouldn't be too long now until my dad would show up here to take me home. This was going to be a night of fear now, not only at the hand of

Barbara, but the threats that would come from my dad. I still wasn't sure why I had been beat so badly. After all, I had no idea what had happened to my sister. There was still the chance that I would get the belt from dad for hurting Susanne. It wouldn't be the first time she would say something short of the truth about me. I think it was how she tried to survive.

Then there was a knock at the door and as it opened there stood my father, all 290 lbs of a big barrel-chested man. Here was a man that with one swift move of his hand had knocked me clear across the room with one blow, and then be ordered back to where he was, to get back handed across the face again for crying from being hit from the first blow.

I too often would hear the words, "Stop that damn crying before I give you something to bawl about!"

Now here he stood, my hope and protection, my safety net of not being beat. Then my father came over and sat down beside me on the couch, putting his arm around me. I wondered then if this was to comfort me, to impress the neighbors, or if it was from his own guilt for letting this goes on for so long. He must have felt uncomfortable sitting there with his arm around me knowing that everyone knew what had been going on for years, and yet he did nothing to stop it. I thought to myself, *What was it he was going to say to these people or to me?*

I no longer had the thought as he said that Barbara felt sorry that she had punished me, because it wasn't me that hit my sister, but the boy down the street named Chuckie. And here was my dad saying, "It is all right. You come home now. This will never happen again. Barbara loves you."

Chapter 16

My First Foster Home

(As we pulled up to the house we were greeted with warm and welcoming smiles from the people standing in the driveway. The state worker lady got out of the car while we waited and she shook the couple's hands, talking with them for a few moments as she glanced over toward us once or twice before coming to open the car door for my sister and me to get out.

I knew who these people were, but I didn't ever recall talking to them much or ever being to their home. They were the pastor and his wife from the church my grandfather went to on Saturdays. The man's name was Greg and his wife was Betty. They were a good-looking couple, full of joy, and they had a little girl named Emilee. The house was the nicest house I had ever seen. The lawn was mowed and well kept and the car was clean and polished, shining in the morning sun. I thought to myself that this was the nicest place I had ever seen or been too. My sister and I were warmly welcomed and they asked us to please come in the house.

Standing there in the entryway I could hardly believe my eyes or my nose. The house was painted white and the living room had the most beautiful furniture I think I had ever seen. The place smelled fresh and clean, almost *too* clean. What a different world I was standing in, thinking for a moment of where I had been only two hours ago when the state social workers came and picked me up.

As our foster parents showed us around the house, I felt uncomfortable and out of place. This was so far from what I had ever experienced. Yes, Grandmother's home was always fresh and clean, but that seemed so long ago and so far away from here. I wondered if she even knew where I was, if anyone had contacted her. I knew that my mother's mom would be worried about me. And then I was feeling bad not even knowing the location of my other sister and two brothers. I hoped that they were alright.

Then the thought of my father came to mind. I hadn't seen him for over a week and wondered if he even had any idea what was happening to me. If he even knew that Barbara was in the hospital or that us kids had been taken away from him. As these thoughts went through my mind I knew the answer to the questions I was asking myself. I didn't know where dad was or what he was doing for sure, but he was no doubt with his girl friend Elaine. He was with her more and more all the time.

"This is where you will be sleeping Charles," my hostess was explaining as she continued the tour of her home. Everything was so nice and in place. She showed me the bathroom and pointed out where the towels and washcloths were kept as I noticed how everything was in order. We were then invited to the kitchen to have some lunch that was already in the oven, smelling good… really good. This was a far cry from what I had been used to. I looked around the room and saw a bowl of fruit on the counter. Betty surely saw me looking as she told me I could have some anytime I wanted. *Really*, I thought.

I had so many things going on in my mind at the same time. Only a few days ago, I was thinking about my little sister and how she had been forced to eat a jar of peanut butter. Once again she had been falsely accused of getting into the cupboard and putting her fingers into the jar and licking her fingers. So Barbara poured a hand full of salt in to the jar and force-fed it to her. She took spoons full and forced it into her mouth, holding her down as she was choked, being beat and thrown into the closet, warned not to come out until it was all eaten. And now, here I stood being offered all I wanted to eat in a peaceful home, no threats or beatings likely to come here, and yet I was feeling most uncomfortable.

The table was set for the four of us and the baby was in the high chair as we sat down to eat. Betty served us lunch while she and Greg made plans for the afternoon. Here, sitting at their kitchen table at lunchtime, were two children thirteen and fourteen years old that came all of a sudden to their doorstep. I'm sure that there were many questions going around in their minds. I thought to myself how much did they know or what the woman from the state even really knew about us. What did they talk about? Then I wished that they didn't know too much, hoping that no one had told them what our house looked like, that we didn't even have any clean clothes to wear, that the sewer was backed up three feet in our house. I was embarrassed thinking that someone had told them the food in the freezer was rotten, or maybe they knew somehow about Barbara and all that she had done to all of us. Now here I was sitting feeling guilty about everything in my life, when Greg spoke up.

"Charles," he asked, "how would you like to go with me this afternoon?"

As we walked through the store Greg pushed the shopping cart down the aisle. He was putting stuff in the cart like new bags of underwear, socks, and under shirts. He seemed to know what would fit me as we moved on to the pants section and Greg asked me to pick out what I would like to wear. I had an uneasy feeling about this. No one had asked me what I wanted to wear… ever. The thoughts flashed across my mind like lightening. I felt as though I was in some kind of a vacuum, unaware of anything else going on around me. I could hear my dad saying to me, "You will wear what I get you and that's it."

Dad, at the beginning of each school year, took us kids school shopping. We got two pairs of pants, some shirts and tennis shoes. The pants were always way too long and, too big around the waist. I had to roll the pants legs up two or three times as not to trip on them walking. Grandpa would tie a cord around my waist to hold my pants up. The kids at school would laugh at me because of the way I was dressed. I wouldn't tuck in my shirt so people wouldn't see how I was holding up my pants. Dad would slap me for not having my shirt tucked in and tell me that he didn't want me looking sloppy.

I really think Greg could sense what I was feeling. He probably saw that I was withdrawn and uneasy and so he walked over and reassured me that everything was alright and said, "You take your time and find exactly what you want to wear."

My sister and I stayed with Greg and Betty for a month. I am sure that our being there put some strain on their relationship. Neither of them ever spoke in a negative tone to me, nor did I ever feel that I was a burden in any way and not welcome. I felt most welcome in the home. However, my sister and I came with a lot of baggage. We never got along. I hated her and had no problem reminding her of the fact. She held the same feelings for me. I was older than she was by almost two years and that could have played some part in the dynamics. She would report to my dad something about me and then look at me with her stupid 'I got you' look while I was being threatened with a beating for being mean to her. On many occasions I would be forced to stand and look at her until I said I was sorry for something she had reported on me. Then she stood there mouthing silent words in my face, taunting me. All the time I was waiting for the moment to grab her long red hair and throw her across the room. Then here was a nice couple, maybe in their mid- to late twenties, probably not married for too long, opening their home to two troubled teenagers that had no idea of what a normal family was, and no concept of right and wrong. Two kids that could look you in the eye and lie without missing a beat. Always fighting, never getting along together.

We all sat down as the social worker was here to give us an update on our situation. Being that Greg and Betty had been so good to us, she was thanking them for having opened their home. I was somewhat excited to be moving on yet at the same time knew that I would miss this couple. Now, with our bags packed with our new clothes, we were headed in the car to our new home - The County Children's Home.

Chapter 17

The County Home

The first thing I remember saying to myself was, *I won't be staying here long,* as we pulled to a stop in front of the County Children's Home.

It was a large brick building surrounded by oak trees in the front. On the side was a fire escape with stairs that led up to the top of the building. There was a parking lot filled with cars to the left and out back of there was a playground filled with swings and other playground equipment. It was clear as we walked up the sidewalk that the social worker had been here often. She opened the door and we entered into a waiting area of sorts. There was an office to the left. The woman sitting behind the desk said hello and made some small talk as we were asked to take a seat. It was more like an order, made to sound nice.

The state lady went directly into the inner office and I was listening to her and a man talk. I couldn't hear what they said. No doubt it was about the two of us sitting out here.

The place had a smell somewhat like the buildings I went to with my mother when I was a small boy. It was an old kind of smell. It looked kind of like those buildings too. The sounds were like those buildings back then also. Everything sounded distant and you could hear it if anything fell to the floor or people talking from a distance.

I really knew I wouldn't like it here. I wondered where my dad was and why he didn't come to get me. It had already been well over a month since I had seen him.

They visited for a short while more in the office when they came out and the lady introduced us.

"Welcome to the County Home," the man said as he told us how he was sure that we would like it here and that if there was anything we needed to please let him, or one of the staff know. I thought, *one of the staff*. I wasn't sure I had heard that term before and knew then I didn't like it. I was convinced that I didn't like him either. Soon the boy's section supervisor greeted me, and the girl's dorm leader welcomed my sister. As I was led down the hallway to the boy's section I, for the first time in my life, felt totally alone. This was all new to me and I was feeling scared inside. I wouldn't let anyone know it though because I had done some growing during the last month. For the first time in my life I had a real sense of strength. It was a new thing to me. I had so much anger built up inside of me. As I walked with this man down the hall way I was sure that I hated him too. He was talking and telling me the rules, saying that nine o'clock was bedtime and lights out. No talking after lights out. You could only get out of bed once in the night to use the bathroom if you needed to. I was taken to my assigned room and introduced to my roommate. This guy was sitting in front of the window looking out when I entered and only then did he turn to look at me. After a few more minutes of getting to know one another we headed to the river to go swimming.

Alright! I thought as we were standing on the bank of the river. I was as close to home right now as I had been in weeks. I loved being at the river and was missing my spot back up the river from the dam where dad worked, but this would do until he came to get me and took me far away from here. There were many kids here. Some lived close by while many of the others lived at the County home too. My roommate made sure that everyone knew where I lived and that we were roomies. I didn't hesitate to jump in and swim to the other side. I was showing off my swimming abilities. I had been swimming for years. Now I was eyeing the rope swing hanging from a large branch out over the deep spot in the middle of the river. I climbed up the cliff and took hold of the rope and swung out and let go. As I popped to the surface I felt a sense of acceptance by the others there. Soon there were people talking to me and asking all kinds of questions: why I was there, where else had I been, had I been in any foster homes and where did I live before the state got me.

The afternoon seemed to pass quickly when someone in the group said it was time to go get ready for supper. So we all walked back toward the home. I was surprised when I saw some of the kids kissing and holding hands. There was even some smoking cigarettes, passing them back and forth, drawing on them real hard and then blowing the smoke out of their lungs. One guy was blowing smoke rings as he was walking. I had never seen this before. Everyone with the smokes hid them in their pants as we went to our room.

It was noisy as I walked into the dining room. There were a lot of people in here. I spotted my sister over in a corner with some other girls as I thought to myself, *I wonder how she's doing?* My roomie had been here for a year and he was showing me everything and telling me the dos and don'ts. His list was different than that of the dorm staff and as it was, I liked his viewpoint much better. Standing in line to eat was new to me also. I mean this was all new, but we had large trays like these at my school as I read the rules on the wall, "NO THROWING FOOD AWAY! EAT WHAT YOU TAKE." I had my food and walked over to the place where my roommate was holding a place for me to sit when a big ugly staff walked up to him and said, "No saving chairs." I heard him say as I sat down "*&^%$."

The meal wasn't that bad. It was a far cry from what Betty had been feeding me. I was thinking to myself,

But at least it hadn't had urine put in it like Barbara had done before at home.

I recalled that we kids were all sitting at the dining room table as Barbara was bringing our food into us. Tonight's meal was goulash. We were all getting sick to our stomachs as the smell was gagging us. She gazed at us with the look of hate and contempt as we were forced to eat our meal. My thoughts about her would come to mind at times when something reminded me of her. I hated her, and over the past few weeks I asked myself why I didn't kill her when I had the chance. No one would have ever known.

The weeks that followed were uneventful other than the walks to the river and that I could blow smoke rings. One day as I was headed to the swimming hole a girl came up and started walking with me. She was telling me about her girlfriend and that this friend had a crush on me. I asked what girl she was talking about and she pointed her out to me. As I turned to see who she was, I got a big smile in return. Now I hadn't thought about any other girls except Sherry Thomas in my life. I still dreamed about her and the time we kissed, and even now, so far away I would think of her when our song, "Just call me angel in the morning, baby," played on the radio. I was in the water keeping cool as the girl waded over to where I was and we talked and spent the day together. Sherry's memory was fading fast. Everyone there had a girlfriend, and now I did too. I was feeling more alive than I ever had in my life. The time at the river was the best and now I had a girlfriend.

I was missing my dad and had made up my mind that the state had not told him how to find me. I didn't understand his absence and didn't believe a word the staff was telling me. So tonight, my partner and I would go to Georgetown and find him. After supper I went to bed with my clothes on. The plan was to meet in the boys' bathroom and then walk down the hall past the dining room. We would go out the side door. As we closed the door behind us I slid a matchbook between the latch and the catch. This way when we got back from Georgetown we would sneak back to bed. No one would ever know that we had left. Down the side streets we ran. I was scared some and I was feeling free at the same time. I had never done this before and I was running as fast as I could. We got to the bridge that crossed the river when someone stopped and gave us a ride for the ten miles to look for dad. I was feeling good to be in my hometown. I had been homesick for my dad and my friends too. I was sure Sherry had a new boyfriend, but I had a girl in Danville waiting to see me in the morning. I knew all the side streets in town and so the cops wouldn't catch me or even see me. I had never thought about the cops before, but tonight if they saw me it would be big trouble. I was a run away from the County Home.

The first place I was going to look for dad was at Elaine Dixon's house. Even if he wasn't there I was sure someone would know where to find him. When I knocked on the door they were surprised to see me. I was asked where I was living and I told them in a foster home. "No, we haven't seen your dad for a couple of weeks," I was told.

The next place I checked was the tavern in Westville. I looked out in the parking lot but dad's car was not there. Now I didn't know where to look or who to ask. So, feeling disappointed, we headed back to the County Home. The door was just as it was when we had left and so we entered the building, headed down the hallway to our rooms and went to bed. I laid there for what seemed hours, thinking about my situation. The more I thought, the more I despised it. The feeling for my dad was growing dimmer by the day as I started to hate him.

Today had been a week since my midnight trip to Georgetown. I was working in the kitchen now and was feeling the home's director breathing down my neck. I never liked him from day one and he was showing his colors to me lately. So I was keeping clear of him and didn't want any part of the paddle he used on some of the boys here. Word was that he swung it fast and hard. Well, he wouldn't get the chance to hit me that was for sure. I had already outsmarted him anyway, and there was a new plan in the works.

Tonight my buddy and I had plans to go visiting our girlfriends. We wouldn't have to go too far this time. They lived in the girl's dorm, second floor, room twelve. We would go out the same way we did before, around the back of the building and up the fire escape and in the window.

So here we were outside after dark once again. I was thinking that I liked this. It was like playing *The Man from U.N.C.L.E.* I'd been doing this for years and was pretty good at getting away. I knew my way around to the fire escape and had been rehearsing it in my head all day. I jumped up caught hold of the ladder and pulled it down. I climbed it up to the window and waited for my partner to catch up. With one leg in the window my heart was beating fast, really fast, and I was now walking down the hall and there was number twelve. I went in slowly and very quietly to bed number four. Then all of a sudden someone screamed, and then someone else and before I knew it the whole second floor was yelling and screaming. I ran fast as I could past the dorm mother's door. Her stupid little dog was barking and jumping on the door. Down the fire escape I went, jumping off the ladder I sped to the door of the hallway. My friend was with me at this point so we sped into our rooms, under the covers, and then the light to my room went on. Just that fast. I had seen a set up before, and this had the smell of a big one.

At breakfast the air was still and heavy. The director was in the dining room and he didn't look happy. In fact he looked mad. His feelers were working and he was on the hunt. *Good luck buddy,* I thought, *you can't pin anything on me.* I had made a clean break. I was in my room and in bed sleeping when the door opened and the light came on. *Don't be looking my way chump!* As breakfast was dismissed there was an announcement over the loud speaker, "All boys from dorm two to the director's office."

Standing up looking ever so innocent, I walked toward the office. The lump in my throat was getting bigger and my head hurt. I had had these feelings before, but somehow today, I wasn't scared. Standing in line with all the others he was walking back and forth in front of us, looking at each one of us with eyes of suspicion. Then all of a sudden he said, "You can all leave now."

My mind was spinning so fast. I was out of here. I had gotten away with it twice now. *You're not so smart big shot,* I thought.

As he continued, "Except you," pointing to my friend, "and you," pointing to me!

As the director walked back and forth he stopped and picked up a large paddle. He told us to bend over and touch the floor. My friend did as he was told and got two hard paddles across his rear end. Next it was my turn. However I said, "You're not hitting me."

As the words came out of my mouth I surprised even myself. He stepped toward me and I warned him that he was not going to hit me, and that if he did my dad would take care of him. As it turned out I got hit three times, each time making sure that I didn't show him that it hurt.

A few days had passed since the paddle incident and I was looking for a way out of here. It would be easy to walk away, however the state social worked would send me up to the boy's ranch. My roommate had spent two years there and he told me I didn't want to take that trip. The thing that really troubled me was that I was here, and my dad hadn't even showed up to see me.

I was sitting in the day room watching a game of ping-pong when I heard my name called to go to the office. I walked down the hall and into the waiting room when I could hear my father's voice coming from the inner office.

I was so happy to see him, yet at the same time I had no trust left in me for him. I asked where he had been and he answered me with a lie. I could always tell when he was not telling the truth. It was in his face - the way his lips would get tight when answering a question; the way he dropped his head forward. And now I was thinking of the time he backhanded me in the face and knocked me down for telling a lie. I had gone looking for him, worried about him and now after all that I had gone through in the last seven years, the last few months and today, he lies to me. We were sitting in the back seat of my dad's car talking. In the front seat was one of the other boys from the group home. Dad had his arm around my shoulder and was telling me how bad he was feeling. He was asking why I hadn't told him what Barbara had been doing to us kids all these years. If only he had known he would have stopped it; telling me how much that he loved me and the other kids. Oh, how things would be different from now on. As he was talking to me there I was thinking in my mind, *I'll never trust you or believe you again.* Then what I never expected would happen, the boy in front seat was pointing a pistol right my head with the hammer cocked back. I was frozen and couldn't move, my dad he was in shock too. I thought for sure I was dead. I knew that the gun was loaded. It was my dad's pistol. He kept it under the front seat. "A gun is worthless if it's not loaded," was dad's saying. Time seemed to stop. We were motionless. I felt hopeless. Then my dad reached slowly forward and took the gun out of the kid's hand, letting down the hammer. All we could do was look at each other. We both knew how close I had come to being killed right there in the back seat of the car.

This would be the last time I would see my dad for a few years, and as we were about to go our separate ways he made me swear to him that I would never tell anyone what had taken place here today. He told me that he would get in to real big trouble if I ever told any one. This wasn't the first time. I had heard this before. "Don't tell anyone or I could get into big trouble," as he had his hands on my shoulders looking down at me So as he got in his car and was driving away, he turned, looked back, and told me that he loved me.

I was sitting in the day room as I heard the voice over the loud speaker order me to the office. "What now?" I thought as I was walking down the hall. "What is it that he wants?"

I had been sitting on the chair for two days already for fighting. It wasn't that I wanted to fight. Actually I didn't like to. The reason was more about the trouble from the staff than the fight itself, but he grabbed my watch and pushed me. I told him to give it back when he laughed at me and said, "What are you going to do about it?"

I said, "Nothing," as I lunged forward and beat the cheese out of him.

Everyone was yelling, "Get him! Don't let him do that to you," as I was on top of him punching his face, but it wasn't me they were cheering on it was the other guy.

I hate this place, I thought as I walked into the office.

Then, there, in the middle of the office floor stood my Grandmother, my mother's mom. She looked at me and said "Oh honey" as she walked over and gave me a kiss oh the cheek. "Why didn't you call grandma?" she said to me. "I would have been here a long time ago for you."

I knew that she meant every word that was said. As she held me, I remember her looking at the director with eyes pleading. This was my mom's mother and ever since mother's death Grandmother had wanted to rescue us kids. This woman stood five foot five and I never recall her being angry, but you didn't mess with her because she got her way. This woman had nothing less than contempt for my father. She knew that he had murdered her daughter and that if given the chance, he would do her harm. This lady had stood toe to toe against my father and begged him to let her raise us children. He would smile looking at her and shake his head no. Today Grandmother would have her way. Take it to the bank!

As we returned from dinner out with Grandmother and Grandfather, sitting in front of the County Home, Grandmother told my sister and me, "I have been praying for years to have you children out of his hands." Today she went on to say, "God has heard me.

How would you like to come with us to Florida to live?"

Was I ever happy to hear those words? Then looking to the front seat I said, "Will they let us go?"

As grandmother turned, looking at her husband, she replied, "Let Grandma worry about that honey."

The very next morning, sitting out front of the County Home in their shiny clean Buick, were my grandparents. Behind the car was the trailer home we had heard about yesterday while out to lunch. Everyone from the home it seemed was out front with us. The staff was telling the kids to stay back, not to climb on the car, while I was telling my friends goodbye. I was happy to be getting out of here, yet I felt a sense of sadness for those I was leaving behind. Now I was sitting in the back seat of the car. I could hear what the home director said to Grandmother as he bent over to look in the window, "I'll see you back here now in two weeks, okay?" My Grandmother looked at him as we pulled away from the curb and didn't say a word.

Chapter 18

Florida '68

Supper was on the table as Grandmother sat down to join us. I had smelled her cooking for hours now and I was ready to eat. Tonight it was pot roast and all the fixings. She had, earlier in the day, baked a peach pie with some of the fruit we got in Georgia on the way down here. It was something, the way she could cook all this food in a trailer home, but she did and I was feeling right at home. I thought it funny that the trailer smelled just like I remembered her house back in Minnesota smelled. Always clean, fresh and well kept. *Yes,* I thought sitting there, *It must be in the Bible, 'cleanliness was next to Godliness'*. I mean she was always saying this when she cleaned and did the dishes.

The trip was a fun experience for me. I didn't miss a thing looking out the car window. We talked with and shared the last seven years with our Grandparents during the long ride. There were times when I would see Grandmother wipe tears from her eyes as we told her what had taken place. On many occasions she would say "Oh honey I didn't know," or "Why didn't you call Grandma?"

Every so often I would say, "You won't believe this but …"

Then this kind lady would say to me, "There isn't anything I wouldn't put past that man."

We shared about being beat with extension cords, mop ringers or anything else Barbara could get her hand at the time. We told Grandmother about the sexual things too. She cried and then she would get a determined look on her face. The same look she had at the county home.

As I sat in the back seat of the car with the window down, the wind blowing in my face, my thoughts were of my little sister. It had been months already since I last saw her there in Georgetown. Now I had tears in my eyes recalling the horrific treatment she had endured at the hand of Barbara. Like the night before her birthday…

Dad had told Barbara to bake her a cake. While everyone was in bed that night, Barbara went down to the kitchen to mess the frosting up. The next morning she called little sister to the kitchen and as she glared in her four year old eyes with threats of a beating, said, "Why did you do this?"

My young sister's response was, "I don't know."
"Chuck," she yelled to my dad, "look at what she did to the birthday cake I made her."

I missed my sister, and sat in the back seat wondering why I didn't kill Barbara when I had the chance at the top of the stairs.

It wasn't like I hadn't seen my grandparents at all during the past seven years. I had. They would always stop by Church Street on their way to Florida and take us out to eat or shopping for clothes. When my dad or Barbara would discover that they were in town, we would be threatened to keep our big mouths shut. This was the warning of what would happen to us if we said anything about how we were living, or how we got treated. My grandparents were never allowed to come in our house. Thinking about it now, I was glad because it was one thing for them to know how we lived, and another if they had seen it. I was even now feeling the embarrassment as I thought about it.

Now, here we sat, far away from all that. As we shared the story with them, I could tell that she was heartbroken by what she was hearing. As I was being loved and cared for by these wonderful people I would recall the way my father would talk about them, how he did all he could to turn us against our mother's parents. The horrible things he would say to cause division in the relationship between them and us. As I thought about it, remembering the way dad looked when he slandered them to me, I hated him. I knew that he was lying then and I knew that he was lying as he turned to look at me that day at the County Home when he said he loved me. As I sat thinking about my dad for a moment, I felt bad for him. If only there was some way I could help him. As I thought about it more, I realized he didn't want my help. He didn't need me. He said he loved me, but that was what he was required to say to his kids. No, my dad was scared and weak and I saw fear gripping him that last day at the County Home.

Standing in the courtroom with Grandfather and my sister, I was thinking about the trip we had taken to get here and about the plans we made last night at the dinner table. We were going to Fort Meyers Beach today to swim and have lunch. Then on the way home we would stop and look at the school where we would be going in the fall.

Then a policeman came out and called our names. Walking into the judge's chambers, I could hear Grandmother, and from the sound of her voice she was going to get her way. I thought to myself, *I've heard this before.*

"But lady", the judge said, "I don't have any say so in this matter. My hands are tied."

Then I could hear Grandmother pleading with them, telling the people in the room that we were in danger if we went back to Illinois. I heard her tell the judge, "You don't have a say so in Illinois, but you sure do here. I want an order of protection for these children and I want it now."

I was imagining her standing toe to toe looking up at him. This woman had lived through much in life. She knew what was right, and she knew how to fight. Never did my Grandmother back down from anyone. I thought for a moment "This is why my father hated her. She wasn't afraid of him"

A few moments later Grandmother walked out of the judge's chamber with a paper in her hand. Not saying a word, she folded it and put it in her purse.

Chapter 19

School in Florida, fall 1968

This was my second time to the Yacht Club and I all ready loved coming here. Yes, South Florida was alright with me. Doing the backstroke in a swimming pool sure was different from the river back home. In fact, back home seemed to get further and further away each day. And the cutie pies sitting around the pool, they were the best. I was sure that the one girl, the real pretty one, was looking at me, and I was looking too. Grandmother said that boys my age were not to be interested in girls. She said that there would be plenty of time for that. Later I reminded her that I had had two girlfriends and had kissed more than that. She would tell me to get my mind on something else. *Jeepers...what,* I thought, *I can't think about girls?*

My grandparents had purchased a new home for us to live in. Across the street was a canal and if you took a boat ride, it would lead to the Gulf of Mexico. It was almost like being at the river. I spent a lot of time there, but I couldn't go swimming because of the coral. It would cut my feet all to shreds is what Grandfather told me. He knew what he was talking about for sure, because a few days later I got a deep cut on my foot.

Yes, I loved being with my grandparents; except for the rules. Everything had a rule. I would remind grandmother that I was not my dad when she would think I was up to something. I usually got the look of "Who do you think you're trying to fool?" I realized that my grandma was a wise woman. She could sniff out a pack of smokes in a minute.

I had fished most every summer for years and had eaten carp, blue gill and catfish, but I couldn't catch a fish out of the canal. I had tried for weeks. They would not bite, and I had tried everything. One morning my neighbor man was standing out on his dock and what he was doing caught my eye. He was pulling in a large gillnet. It was full of fish. I ran over and asked him if I could help. There were all kinds of fish. He said that the fish swim into the net at night and get caught and can't back out. He also told me why I had not been catching any fish and suggested that I get a spear. When we were finished taking the fish out of the net, he sent me home with ten large fish called Jacks.

Grandfather was excited to see the fish I had. He called Grandmother and she came out with the camera for a picture. First, I held them up and then it was Grandfather's turn. We had a good meal of fish for supper that night and I was feeling right at home. When grandmother put the pie on the table she informed us that we were going shopping in the morning for school supplies. We would also go and take a tour of the junior high school we would be attending in a few weeks.

Summer is never over in south Florida and today was no different, other than I was on the bus headed for school. I was actually excited about it, and so when we arrived I jumped off the bus and headed for my locker. I had been here two weeks ago for the tour and already knew the place pretty well. The thing that was cool to me was that all the hallways and lockers were outside. They were only covered with a roof. So it really didn't seem like school at all.

The first day went well and was uneventful. I met the teachers and got my schoolbooks and enjoyed playing ping-pong during lunch break. There was all the talk about tomorrow and I sensed a buzz and an uncomfortable feeling in the air. It seemed to be all because the blacks were being bused in from North Fort Meyers to go to our school. They called it desegregation. I really didn't get the problem everyone was talking about. My partner in the county home was black and we were good friends. It was the two of us that went looking for my dad that night, and we both stood in line to get the paddle for going up to the girl's dorm. His sister, she was sweet as could be. We even made out a few times at the river.

The talk was all about the blacks coming to school today as we headed for the second day. I thought it was stupid the way people were talking. To me it was as dumb as the rule that the boys and the girls had to sit on different sides of the bus. As I was thinking about this, it was troubling to me. I knew the feeling in the air all to well. I had felt it myself many times and now I was seeing it in other people's faces. It was fear - and now it was being mixed with something else - hate.

I stepped off the bus and headed into the building. I noticed people were all lined up, standing with their backs to the walls, all the way down the hall on both sides. People were talking, but in a low voice, almost in whispers. At the end of the hall stood last year's football team. They all had on their school letter jackets, giving each other high fives, talking how they had beat the black's football team last year. They were so sure that there was no room on the team for the new students. I stood there watching and listening to everything. Hearing what was being said and seeing the faces, the message was not the same. They were afraid too. I stood there for another moment and then I asked this one kid, "What are you scared of?"

The whole team turned and looked at me with eyes of disapproval and answered, "Not you."

I walked away and turned back over my shoulder and said, "See you later, BROTHER."

One bus pulled up, then another, and another. There were four in all. The new students stepped off the bus and walked toward the door. It was clear to me as I looked down the hall that they were having many of the same feelings that I saw in the white kids - fear and uncertainty. I was sure many of them didn't want to be here either. As they started down the hall, it was very quiet and still. The air was filled with fear. The fear of something new, being in a strange place, walking down a hall surrounded by others with the same uneasy feelings and fear of possible harm. And then, not even thinking about what I was about to do, I started down the hall saying "Hey, how you doing? Welcome to your new school... Give me five brother... Hey how you doing lady? Come on in."

The ice was broken. People started to move from standing along the walls and we were all headed to class.

I had never played football in my life, but here I was standing in line doing toe touches with the rest of the team. I didn't really have a desire to be here, but I didn't want to go home either. Home was nice, and my grandparents were as good and caring to me as people could be. They loved me, no doubt. Thing was, I was fifteen. I had so many things going on in my life, so many thoughts. Things seemed to move so quickly through my mind. Things I had never thought possible. I wasn't scared. No one was beating me. I had friends and my girlfriend Vicky. Life was good. But I had a sense that something was missing.

"Hey you, start running!" the coach was telling me. Seemed that I had hardly finished another twenty-five push-ups and now I was having to run laps. I ran as fast as I could, wanting to keep up with the others. I had decided that I wouldn't be last and that was my determination. I was so out of breath when practice was over. Standing in the shower all I could think about was dinner and going to bed.

Seems that sitting in a classroom was about the most boring thing I have ever had to do. It wasn't that I didn't like it so much. It was alright. I didn't seem to get it. I studied, did the home work, but somehow I couldn't retain the material. At test time I seemed to go blank. I would be in a vacuum. I couldn't concentrate and this all reflected in my grades. My mind was always moving so fast. It would go from one place to another like lighting. As I sat here looking at the teacher trying to listen, the kid next to me said, "Don't come to football today or I will kick your %$#"

I said, "What are you talking about?"

"I don't want you or your black friends on my team," he answered.

So the rest of the day this was all I could think about. I couldn't shake it. I didn't want to get into trouble. I wasn't scared of him. It was the trip to the office I didn't want to take. Grandmother had already warned me about that. Then I decided I would go to practice. He wouldn't stop me.

Getting my clothes changed in the locker room that afternoon was uncomfortable as the other players were saying, "You're going to get your %$# beat if you walk out to the field. Go home and take your friends with you, you %$#@ lover."

Seemed odd to me that they wouldn't say anything to the brothers about playing, but they had me in there sights. So I waited and took my time going out the back door to the field. Being last would only mean a lap. Fighting and getting in trouble could mean back to the county home. When everyone had left the locker-room I headed outside the door and it closed and locked behind me. As I turned the corner to go to the field there was Darin Megan in the center of the circle of other players, waiting for me. He was ready to fight and was bouncing on his toes getting the approval of the other boys. He was saying, "Come on you! I'm going to smash your face, you &^%$ lover. Go home! I don't want you on my team."

I walked over to go around him not wanting to get into trouble for fighting, but the circle got tighter. There was no way out. So without any warning I rushed him, knocking him to the ground. I had my arm wrapped around his neck and was pounding the snot out of him. I hit him and hit him as hard as I could until he started crying like a baby. I punched him some more and then I let him go. When I got up everyone else was gone. Then standing there, I was thinking about how bad I felt about what I had done to this kid. I didn't want to fight. He pushed it, and now I am feeling guilty. I didn't like feeling this way. *The punk got what he had coming,* I said to myself, and *I'll give him some more if he wants.*

Still, I was sad.

Chapter 20

The Lie Detector Test

I could tell from the way Grandmother was looking at Grandfather that the telephone call was about me. The social worker had called and said that the court had ordered us back to Illinois. We had to be there in two weeks. School was out so we wouldn't be missing any of that. Seemed that there was going to be a court hearing about us kids, and all five of us had to be there. It would be nice to see the others. I hadn't seen my one brother or my other sister since that morning when the police and the state came and took us away from the house.

I liked living with my Grandparents, but because I was so out of control I would not be coming back to Florida with them. I couldn't blame them for anything. I was living two lives. We agreed that it would be better if I stayed in Illinois. I was smoking and leaving the house in the middle of the night while everyone was sleeping, going out and being with my friends. I would sneak around and was looking in people's cars and taking stuff. Anything I could find. There wasn't a thing I needed. I simply like the action and the thrill of what I was doing. Lying in the dark, looking out to see if anyone was around. Then striking and getting away. I had been doing this for years and I really liked it. The police about got me once, but I hid and they didn't find me. Talk about a thrill. I seemed to need the drama, mixed with the fear and excitement of getting away. I would never get caught. I felt that I would probably do this all my life. Grandmother didn't know everything I was up to, but I was sure that nothing would have surprised her. How I recall the way she use to say, "You can't pull the wool over my eyes," and then follow it up by reminding me that she knew my father all to well.

Funny, I thought, that she could see my father in the way I behaved. And she was right - I was up to no good. Though she didn't know exactly what it was, she knew. We had been in Illinois for two days when we were sitting in the courthouse. I didn't see my dad, but I knew he was there because I had heard someone say to Grandmother that he was down the hall. The social worker assured her that he was not allowed to see us until after the court hearings. Then a man came out and said to follow him. Grandmother said that it was alright and she would see me in a little while.

He led me in to a small room and asked me to take a chair. He explained that the machine on the table was a polygraph machine. He said that some people call it a lie detector because it can tell if you're telling the truth or not. He then connected me with some wires. One was on my finger with a clip and another was around my chest.

"I am going to ask you some questions, and I want you to tell me no when I ask if your name is Charles," he said.

He asked me some other questions too. "This," he said, "is to get a base line. Now relax and breathe normally."

Then he asked me questions about everything that went on at Church Street. "Did I see this and that?" He wanted to know if I saw something or if someone had told me to say it. He asked me questions I had already spoken to the caseworker about. He asked me about my dad and about my sister. He wanted to know if Barbara had burned my little sister's arm with cigarettes and if I saw her do it.

"Did Barbara force your sister to eat a jar of peanut butter mixed with a box of salt?"

"Did she force you to eat food she had &%$@# in it?" he asked. "Did Barbara beat you with a two by two? Why was the food locked up?"

Then he asked the ugly questions. The hard to answer ones… The things about the bedroom…

This went on for a while and then we were through. When we were back in the courtroom, the judge then ordered us not to talk about anything we were asked or anything we had said with anyone until he saw us again. Then he ordered that our father was to have no contact with us until further notice.

"Do you understand me sir?" he asked my dad.

After what would be my last meal with grandmother and grandfather for some time, we went back to the courthouse. As we were entering, there were dad and Barbara sitting a short distance from us. She looked at me with the same old look of hate she always had, and I thought to myself, *I could have killed you, you nasty %$#@.* I turned and gave her a sarcastic looking smile. At times I wished that I would've killed her that night. The hate I had for her was colder now than it had ever been. She could have dropped dead on the spot and I would have walked around her. The one thing Barbara taught me was hate. I had plenty of it too. It was all for her. The day I beat the boy at school it was her face I saw on him as I hit him and punched his face in.

We had all taken our seats when the judge walked in to the courtroom. The lawyers went forward and spoke for a moment and then the judge said, "The children will remain in the care of the state until further notice. All records in this matter are to be sealed," and then he slammed the gavel down. It was over.

When left the courthouse, we had been told that we could, if we wanted to, visit with our dad for a few minutes. So standing beside his car we talked for a while as he told how much he loved us and missed us. Then his now wife Barbara said, "Let's go."

He got in to the car and drove away. It seems that after all these years we thought that they were married. That was one more lie in a web of deception and deceit that I had been made to believe for years. As they drove off he didn't even look back. And I was headed for a new chapter in my life. I was going to another foster home.

Chapter 21

Riots, Hippy Chicks and The War

Working at my new job at the restaurant was great fun and I liked washing dishes and bussing the tables. I was working full time. For a high school junior I was doing alright. There were plenty of cute waitresses too and I got along with all of them. The manager said he liked my energy, and because I was really fast at the dishwasher, soon I would be working on the grill with him showing me how.

I had been living with my new foster parents for many months now. They were really nice people. They told me that I could work all the hours I wanted at my new job as long as I went to school on time and saved half of my paychecks. This all seemed good to me, so I worked every chance I had. My foster mother opened a savings account for me and I loved handing my check over to her knowing that she took real good care of my money. After another month or so I started to buy U.S. Savings Bonds. I liked the thought of spending thirty-seven fifty for a fifty dollar bond. That seemed like good math to me. Saving my money was fun and it was adding up fast.

The Timmons had cared for foster children for many years, and were well suited for the job. This couple had two children of their own and one adopted daughter.

Over the years, fifty or more kids with needs had passed through their home. Each one was treated with love and compassion. I was treated no differently. Mrs. Timmons was a stay at home mom. Mr. Timmons was a fireman and worked for the University of Illinois. He would work twenty-four hours on and forty-eight off. This gave me opportunity to visit him at the fire station, and occasionally I did.

The fire station was only two blocks from the University of Illinois and where all the action was. So I would ride my ten-speed bike over to see Mr. Timmons and then go hang out with the anti-war people and the hippies on the steps of the university buildings protesting the war in Vietnam.

School was a breeze. Not that my grades were any good. They were not. On the other hand I got along well at school, had money in my pocket, and had a new girlfriend. Terri and I only had one class together, but I would run to see her after every class and walk her to her next. Sometimes we would meet somewhere in between and hang out for a few minutes. I had been warned more than once about kissing in the hallway, and holding hands with Terri. I would just tell the teachers that what the world needed was more love. Somehow I got away with it. Funny thing, two of our teachers were engaged and they were seen many times kissing between classes too, so this somehow was our justification. Not being allowed to hold hands in school was, I thought, as stupid as boys and girls sitting on opposite sides of the school bus.

On the evenings when I didn't have to go to work, I spent my time at the University of Illinois bowling alley. I was either bowling or playing pool and, every chance I had, was hanging out with the babes. This was a fun place to hang out. I knew several of the college girls because they worked with me at The Howard Johnson's. Seemed that everyone was protesting these days, or marching in a civil rights parade. The hippy chicks either smelled like patchouli or grass, sometimes both, and they carried signs that read STOP THE WAR, GIVE PEACE

A CHANCE. I used to joke, and say give me a chance.

The hippy guys seemed to have their own set of issues. For them it was more about the war or the talk of Canada. I didn't give any of this much thought, but the hatred caused me sadness. I really didn't get it. On the weekends there were always the riots going on in the north end of town. People were forced to stay on their own side of the street. Here in Illinois people were having the same fears and hatred and as they did in Florida. They were fighting about civil rights. Blacks were on one side and whites on the other. I thought it was stupid. I had plenty of other things to do and think about than fighting over the color of a person's skin. It did seem though everywhere I lived it was the same thing - civil rights. I wasn't sure what the big deal was anyway. I mean, I got along with the black folks. Really, I like them sometimes even better than some white folks.

Spring was here and I was feeling restless. The Timmons continued to be great people and I, up to that point in my life, had never known any finer. But I was getting restless and agitated. I wanted to go and do my own thing and my mind was moving so fast all the time. Really I didn't know what it was, but I had the desire to travel. Get on the road. Go out and party and hang with the babes. After all, I had girlfriends since I was eleven and besides, I needed some excitement, some drama. Something was stirring up inside me. I was restless and on the move. I wanted to hit the road, get out on my own. So I went to the bank early one morning, cashed in all my savings bonds, and withdrew all the cash from my savings. Then, without saying a word to Terri or to anyone, I packed my bags and caught a Greyhound bus headed north. I was filled with excitement and adventure, and a little mischief. For the first time in my life I was on my own. No one was telling me what to do and there was no one to threaten me. *Yes,* I thought, *I liked this*. So I lay back in the seat and settled in for the bus ride to Minnesota. I didn't really have a plan other than I would look up my old man and see what he had to say for himself.

Chapter 22

Uncle Ron's help

Arriving at the Greyhound bus station in St. Paul brought back memories of my being there with my mother only eleven years earlier. Oh, how much things had changed. My mother would never have allowed the things that had gone on in my life the past eleven years. I found myself missing her again. I hadn't done this for many years, and now I felt that it would be nice if I could see her. I recalled sitting at this same counter having hot cocoa before getting on the bus that day for Rochester. I wondered for a moment if mother would even know me now if she could see me. I thought about how she might look. Then I realized I only had a glimpse of a memory of her lying in the casket that day. I remembered that a woman had screamed because she thought mother had opened her eyes and looked at her. It was a reflection from her glasses but it was real enough. Then for a moment, like I was somehow cast back in time, I heard the man over the loud speaker announce, "Rochester, Winona, Des Moines and all points south, gate two." I had to fight back a tear.

Now, here I was in Minnesota by myself and no one in the world knew I was here. Everything I owned was in a flight bag or on my back, and I had almost two thousand dollars hidden in my pants. I was feeling free somewhat and realized that I didn't even have a plan. I knew that my dad lived here somewhere and that I wasn't even sure I wanted to see him, so looking up my Uncle Ron's phone number, I gave him a call.

My uncle Ron had been in my life as long as I could remember. He had come to visit us in Georgetown once and it was there that I first met his wife, my Aunt Jan. He had even watched us kids for a while when mother was alive, so he was someone that I trusted. For a moment I thought about how I used sneak out the bedroom window and play with my friends while uncle thought I was asleep. Seemed like so long ago now and so much has happened in my life. I was hoping that my uncle would be glad to see me after all that had taken place. Georgetown seemed so far away yet so clear in my mind, and my dad gave up his rights to his children to keep Barbara and to avoid prison.

It wasn't long after I hung up from talking to him that he was there to pick me up. Driving to his home I was sharing with him some of what I had been up too for the past few years. He listened with interest and we were still talking when we pulled in to his drive way. Ron and Jan made me feel at home and set me up in a room in the basement.

Over the next few weeks Uncle set me up for some job training where he worked as a counselor and job coach. I was learning some job skills and things like that. I felt good when people would say to me, "Oh, you must be Ron's nephew."

I felt like I had some favor. It was the first time that I could think of that I liked school. One afternoon my uncle said that he thought it would be wise to contact Family Services in Illinois, and let them know where I was and that I was alright. He also contacted the social services people in Minnesota asking for their help to let me stay there. My uncle was concerned for me and didn't want me to get into any kind of trouble.

I had seen my dad on a few occasions when he would come over to Ron's house. I wasn't really too excited about visiting with him, but felt some kind of obligation towards him. I really didn't know why. I mean, the last two times I saw him were not very exciting, one being that day at the court house when he left with his Barbara in the car, and then the day he begged me not to talk about the gun incident at the county home. No, he didn't seem overly excited to see me now, and I had a feeling then that I could never trust him.

On one afternoon he came and picked me up from Ron's house. We went driving around and he was showing me places we used to live and that kind of stuff. He looked like he had something on his mind all afternoon. Then he pulled into a parking lot in the housing projects, this is where he ended up living after all these years. I thought, *the projects…*

Walking with him into the house brought back immediate memories of Georgetown; Tthe way it looked, the sounds and the smell. And there was Barbara. She looked the same, still didn't have teeth in her mouth, and now she had four kids. Two of them I had never seen. One was my little half brother and the other was the baby girl she had that night in Georgetown, when I ran to get her help. When she finally turned to speak to me, I saw two things in her eyes that I was all too familiar with. One was the hate. She loathed me and always had. The other was fear. She was afraid of me, and my being there had already taken its toll on her. I saw it in her face.

The social services department in Illinois was not at all happy with me. They sent a court order to Minnesota and had me arrested as a run away. That same afternoon I stood before a judge by myself for the very first time. He slammed his gavel down and said, "Back to Illinois with him."

They took me to a waiting cell and they were looking for a policeman to take me to the airport. I didn't know what was waiting for me back in Illinois and I was sure I wasn't going to like it. Two cops drove me to the airport and I was hoping that the one on the passenger side wasn't going to be the one to fly me back. I thought to myself, *this cat is full of himself*. I didn't like him.

Here I was waiting to board a plane back to Illinois. I didn't want to go back, for no particular reason. I simply wanted to stay in Minnesota. As we boarded the plane the cop said to me, "You have a good flight Charles," and walked off the plane.

The flight was great but I wasn't quite sure what exactly was going on. It didn't seem real that I was put on a flight without supervision. Well, I had some lunch and ordered a drink and was making the best of my situation. The stewardess came with my drink and gave me exactly what I had ordered, minus the booze. Oh well, I was not going to let that get me down. I hadn't ever had a martini anyways.

As the plane was making its approach to land in Chicago, my heart was beating hard. Would there be someone to walk me to the next plane?

I walked off the plane and stayed close to a group of people I had been talking to during the flight. I wanted to appear as though I was with them. Looking around there was no one waiting for me. I was now supposed to go and catch another flight to Champagne/Urbana. I wouldn't be catching that flight however. I looked at the monitor for departures and decided to return back to Minnesota. I found a seat in the terminal and got a hundred dollar bill out from under the inside sole of my shoe. Cashing in the ticket I had and with some added money, I had another ticket for a flight back to Minnesota.

Chapter 23

Grandma and the Pool Hall '71

Standing outside in the early morning at Grandmother's, I thought about the first time I had been to Washington. It was the summer of '67 when my cousin Robin and I took our first airplane ride together. We had come to visit Grandma and Grandpa, my father's parents. They lived outside of town at the foot of Mount Rainier and we had a wonderful summer here. It seemed so long ago that we had fished and went swimming in the Tilton River together, and had taken our first trip to the ocean. It had been only four years ago that I was here and I had wanted to stay here then. Man it seemed like so long ago.

Now I was a run away, wanted by the state of Illinois. Thinking about it, I really didn't care. Actually I liked the drama and excitement of it all. But on another level, I was still sad and empty inside wondering what would ever become of me. Thinking about it now I wondered how different my life would have been if I had continued on to the social workers.

Grandfather Dudrey had died in '69 when I was in Florida with my other grandparents. Now it seemed funny that my Grandmother had a boyfriend. Not only that, but they were going to get married soon. And if things couldn't get any stranger in my life, I would be the best man at the wedding, and my great-grandmother would be the bridesmaid. Bill was a fine man and he loved my Grandma. I liked to hear him call her by her nickname, Sweets, and Grandma seemed to approve. More than that, I was sure she liked it.

Morton was a small logging town and everyone knew everyone else. It didn't take but a few days before I was out and about, meeting the kids in town. I had, it seemed by now in my life, been more places and done more things than many of the kids my age. This had its advantages being new here, and I liked all the attention I was getting. I spent every day shooting pool and listening to the jukebox. Every so often I would step out back and smoke some grass with someone. It was something, I thought, that they didn't know what a nose hit was. All my hanging out at the University had paid off and I could roll a joint with one paper without tearing it. Cool.

I had already found a small job working for the lady who owned the second hand store. I liked having cash money, and I didn't have to tap in to the cash I still had put away. I was calling it my running cash. To add to the drama, I was wanted by the law in Illinois, and really didn't think too much about it. I knew that when I turned eighteen there was nothing they could do to me anymore, and I had only a few months to go before my birthday. I hadn't really done anything in Illinois to go to jail for except leave without their permission.

Really, as I thought about it, I didn't really care what the social workers had to say or what they thought. Who were they to tell me anything? I had decided that I was old enough to do what I wanted and if they didn't like it, so what. I was on my own and doing better than I ever had. I liked Washington and I thought that someday I could live here, but for now I needed to stay off the radar. So I spent days playing pool and listening to the jukebox and singing along with Janis Joplin and Smoky Robison's, *Tears of a Clown*.

One day, out of the blue, I decided to go back east. I would find a place to live and get some employment. I was feeling restless and bored, and wanted to hit the road. So with only a little warning, I said so long to everyone and caught a train back east. I discovered that I loved traveling and being on the road and I was getting to be quite the man of the world. Sitting in the dining car having breakfast one morning, I kept playing my life over and over in my mind. The more I thought about it the more I just wanted to keep on the road going from town to town. Seemed somehow I was running from more than a social service office. It went deeper than that; much deeper. But I wasn't sure what it was.

When I got back I learned that my dad and Barbara had separated and he was managing some apartment buildings in St. Paul, two blocks off the strip. This was where all the action was happening. So I ended up there, renting a ground floor one bedroom apartment with a private entrance and a porch. The rent was easy, at seventy-five dollars a month, and so I started furnishing my first home. I had purchased my very first vehicle, a pick-up truck, and I would put it to use. I drove around the upper class, well-to-do part of town and hauled stuff to the dump for people. I was doing pretty well at this little business. Where ever I drove I looked for an opportunity to haul something. After awhile I decided to save some cash on the dump fees, so I unloaded my truck out behind some old buildings on the other side of town. One day, on a vacant lot, I dumped a load of junk that I had picked up behind a garage for some people only a few blocks away. Some guy saw me do it and started to chase me in his car. I was driving through the alley and down side streets, but the citizen kept following me. He was honking his horn and flashing his lights. He must have been watching too much TV thinking he could catch me. I think it was the flying across intersections that finally put an end to the chase and I ditched him. He wasn't having as much fun as I was and probably wished he hadn't chased me in the first place. I saw two of his hubcaps rolling down the street as I looked into the rear view mirror.

"Chump," I thought, "get yourself some business."

I thought to myself that yes, I had some operation going. I was in the trucking business. But with the price of gas going up to fifty-six cents a gallon I had to cut some costs. So I relied on an old system I had learned from my dad - the siphon hose. I had filled many cans of gas from the company truck for dad, so now I had this all figured out and was doing well. I would go out early in the morning, fill up my gas cans, and have enough fuel for the day.

Chapter 24

Quaaludes, Arsenic and Suspicion

I first met Poppy in the county jail. I had been reading about him for weeks in the local newspapers. *Man Arrested for String of Safe Jobs.* He had been hitting businesses all over the state, prying open safes or cutting them open with a cutting torch. I was getting bailed out of jail that afternoon and Poppy pleaded with me to make some phone calls and help him get out too. I said that I would and we could go make some money together. I had been sitting here for a probation violation. One year ago I had been arrested for credit card theft, and I had been sentenced to five years in prison. The sentence was set aside if I completed a stay at a community corrections program. The program was started as an alternative to prison for first time offenders and I qualified. I wouldn't have ever been arrested or charged with a crime, but I took the fall for my dad and his girlfriend.

My dad's girlfriend was a widow for a second time and she continued to receive credit cards in the mail in the name of her late husband. She and her husband had been married only a short time when he died and left her a home and a farm. She and dad met while he was still with Barbara, and I thought that he had made a good decision leaving Barbara for her. She was good looking, could carry on a conversation, and had some class. It was a far from cry from Barbara's body odor and filthy mouth.

My dad would drive down to her house every night after work and then make the return trip back to St. Paul in the morning, some seventy-five miles each way to go to work.

One weekend Susan invited me down to her house with dad. She said that she had a younger sister that she wanted me to meet, and we could all go out dancing for the weekend, I said, "Oh ya!" and accepted.

It was no little secret that I was a self-proclaimed criminal. I had, since moving back to Minnesota, been wheeling and dealing, robbing and stealing. It was the drama and the action of it all that drove me. I loved the fast pace, the excitement. My senses were keen and I could spot trouble or a threat before it even came my way. I was able to scan a room or a crowd of people and be aware of everyone and everything that was going on. One day, Susan showed me a hand full of unused, unsigned credit cards. I was sure that my dad put her up to it, but it wouldn't have mattered either way. I said, "Let's do it."

She and my dad didn't seem as sure as I was about it. Or maybe they were scared of getting caught. I made it clear that I would not involve them if anything ever went wrong. I would never tell. I would take the hit. So with that out of the way, I said, "Let's sign the cards and let's go shopping."

I was having fun shopping and was feeling like the big spender. Dad would sit in the car, Susan and I would go in to the store and fill the cart with the things we had talked about. We were furnishing her home. Once at the checkout, I would go into script, take out my card and pay for the merchandise like I had been doing it all my life. Then I would thank the cashier, telling them to have a nice day and met Susan at the door. We then walked out to the waiting car. I was full of myself and ready to do it again. Yes, I had a game going and liked the drama. I figured that we should use the cards until they wouldn't accept them any longer. At the next stop, Dad and Susan went shopping. They would fill the cart with what they wanted, then would walk out to the car and tell me where the cart was. I would go in, present the card, and get the merchandise. We had been doing this for weeks covering two states.

One night while Susan and I were shopping, a security man came up to me and said to follow him, as he took a hold of my arm. I could see Susan looking my way so I gave her the sign to leave. The store detective walked me up toward his office and was asking me questions about my name and whose card it was I was using. As we were about to enter his office, I said that I needed to use the restroom and he said it was alright. I went in the door while he waited outside, and then immediately turned around ran out the bathroom door, pushing and knocking the store detective down. I ran out the emergency exit, down the fire escape to the outside of the building and never turning back, I ran as fast as I could. I then walked into a motel and called a cab to take me where Susan would be waiting if something went wrong. Good plans make for a good job I told her. She wasn't so sure. She asked me if I was scared, and I assured her that I had been doing this all my life and that I liked the action. After talking together with my dad we all decided it best if I left town for a while. So, the next morning, I went to the airport and caught a flight south.

The flight down was good. Florida was as nice as I had remembered it to be. I drove past the house I used to live in with my grandparents. They had moved back to Minnesota some time ago after the court deal in Illinois. Now I was thinking about them, and how much I loved them.

It was now weeks since I knocked down the detective and ran out of the store. I liked being back on the Gulf Coast. I had found a job in a grocery store and was living with some friends I knew from high school. I was doing pretty good here and from time to time I would laugh to myself, thinking about the scam I had pulled and gotten away with. I craved the action and liked the traveling.

I remembered, when I was growing up in Georgetown, thinking that I would like to be a hit man, a spy or even a secret agent like the guys on *The Man from U.N.C.L.E.* or *Simon Templar*. Yes, I could be the Saint. I recalled how I use to dream about this. I knew that what I had been doing was wrong, but it didn't seem to matter to me. I was used to this life and I felt alive and free. I liked what I was doing, running around with friends, hanging with the cuties, and if I needed some cash, I went and got some real easy.

I had gotten word that my dad wanted me to call him, so I went to a pay phone and dialed his number. It seemed that the State of Minnesota Bureau of Criminal Apprehension had a warrant out for me. They knew that I was the one who had charged thousands and thousands of dollars on the credit cards. They told dad that if I would come back and turn myself in, they would be easier on me than if they had to find and arrest me. *They have to find me first*, I thought.

Then dad reminded me of what I had said about if I got caught, not to implicate anyone else. I assured him that I would do as I said I would. As I hung up the telephone, I shook my head thinking that my old man was weak.

"So tell me about your relationship with Susan," he asked as I was being interviewed at the jail. "How long have you known her?"

"Did you know her husband Carl? Did you know that his death is being investigated?"

"Tell me about Robert. Did you know him? Have you ever heard anyone talk about his death?"

"Did you know that they both died suddenly? Did you know that their deaths both took place in less than a year?"

The questions kept coming about things I had no knowledge about. I knew that there had been an investigation going on, but I didn't know anything about it.

"Tell me what you know about arsenic?" he asked. "Have you ever known anyone to have any?"

Interesting, I thought. Three of the same people that were there in the house the morning my mother was killed were together again and lived in the same house only a few months ago, Barbara, her brother Walter and my dad.

"What a coincidence," I thought. Now I'm being questioned about two other people who are dead.

"We think that Susan had something to do with the death of her husband… not one, but two," he went on.

"We wanted her to take a polygraph test," he told me, "but she was so high on Quaaludes that the test came back inconclusive."

Now this was all becoming familiar to me. I didn't say a word to him. That wasn't my style. I did know something about arsenic, though. Dad had a vial in his safe. And Quaaludes, oh yes. There was that night in Duluth when dad or Susan slipped one in to my coffee. I remembered that night alright. I had gone to the bathroom at the Chinese restaurant we were eating at. When I came back to the table I sipped some coffee and recalled how I said, "Those Chinese make some strong coffee."

I woke up the next morning still in the car. Yes, this detective wanted something on Susan, and he wanted it bad. He wouldn't get it from me.

"You know if you had permission to use those credit cards we can't charge you with anything. Did Susan help you use them? You can make this all go away now if Susan gave you permission."

"No," I said.

Well, it didn't take long and Poppy and I were up to doing some jobs together. As soon as he could, he wanted to pay me back the bail money I had raised to get him out of jail. I really thought it funny. He would read the phone book while sitting on the toilet, looking for a place that might have a safe. Car dealers and restaurants were always good targets, so we planned to do a car dealer on Saturday night. That was when the safe would have the most cash. The banks were not open on weekends so this was the best time to hit them.

We were in the car dealership using pry bars and peeling back the steel on the safe when all of a sudden we hit a tear gas wall liner in the safe. We were choking and gasping for air. We took turns running back to the door for air and then holding our breath while working on the box. Finally we had the money and headed out. We crossed the field to the waiting car. We had made a clean break, were heading back to town and making plans for our next caper.

Chapter 25

Prison and the Con Job

"Someone saw us! Someone saw us!"

That's what Poppy was yelling as he dropped the cutting torch and headed for the door. We had almost cut through the safe, when someone looked in the window of the tractor dealership and stared right at us. It was Sunday morning early and all these farmers were supposed to be in church. Now we were spotted and needed to make a run for it.

I got behind the wheel of my car and headed for the freeway. I was feeling good to have made it this far without seeing a cop. My heart was pounding like all the other times at this stage in the game. Get away before you get busted. Get as far as you can. Blend in to the flow of traffic. I would soon be crossing the state line back in to Minnesota as fast as I was driving. Looking at the speedometer I was driving over a hundred and picking up speed. We had a close one back there I thought looking into the rear view mirror. That would be all I needed, going back to jail. My probation officer didn't like me anyway. She would rather have me out of her hair I'm sure.

Man that was scary. My heart was beating faster than I was driving, and then, pulling up beside me was a state trooper. The cop was talking on his radio and looking right at me. I pushed the gas pedal to the floor, but he stayed right beside me. He had one hand on the steering wheel and in the other he was holding a shotgun with the strap wrapped around his forearm pointing it right me. "Pull over," he said over a loud speaker, "now!"

I had so many thoughts going on in my mind. I was feeling sorry for myself and that was not a good feeling. I was scared that we had been busted and I had no choice except to pull over or get shot. Sitting there in the car waiting for the cops to arrest us seemed like a long time. Time enough to be disappointed in myself, or more like being mad that I had been caught. It took only a few moments and there were other cops all around us with guns out pointing at us. It wasn't too long after that we were sitting in the county jail. I was in trouble. Real big trouble, and Poppy knew it too.

It had been only a month ago that Poppy and me met in another jail, and here we were both being charged with burglary. We should have been happy with last night's safe job. We netted some good cash. But no, we wanted more. It was fun living in the fast lane, pulling a wad of money out of your pocket to pay for something. Now it looked like we were going to get more than we expected. I wasn't at all feeling so great anymore. There would be no talking my way out of this one and dad wouldn't be here with bail money.

No, not this time. We were caught in the act. We were going to prison.

The drive to the State Men's Reformatory was a quiet ride. I didn't have much to think about. I was disappointed in myself for being in this situation and now going to prison. Sure enough I had made the decisions that got me into this mess, and yet I have to admit I had some good times in the process. The problem was that I got caught and this was all I was thinking about. I wasn't having fun anymore. This wasn't in the script.

Poppy plead guilty sooner than I did and so he had already been in the reformatory about a month before I got there. There he was, standing and waiting for me when I walked in the front gate. He had already picked up a new skip in his walk and had hooked up with some partners. He had sure made himself at home and was making the best of it. He said that he would see me in the chow hall later and would have me some more smokes. As he handed me a pack there inside it was a joint too. This place couldn't be all that bad I thought and I hadn't seen anything that really surprised me. I had met some of these guys in the county jail that had been here before and said the place was pretty laid back. They were right.

My cell was freshly painted and so that made it homey. Compared to when I slept in the closet as a kid, this wasn't so bad. It a little more room. My television would be here in a few days and dad said that he would bring my guitar down sometime in a few weeks. So I had decided that this would be home for a while and that I would get as comfortable as I could. I came in to the place with some money from my last safe job so I could go to the canteen and buy about whatever I needed.

This prison had open yard, so when I wasn't working I could come and go pretty much as I wanted. I would learn my way around inside here pretty fast. Actually the place wasn't that bad, and so it wasn't long that I was smoking weed every day. I had made some friends and had been doing some wheeling and dealing so I did the best I could under the circumstances. I went to the weight yard and found that I liked pumping iron too. So I purchased some vitamins and some protein supplements from the canteen and was feeling good with the results I was getting.

The food in the chow hall was great. On Sundays it was steak or ham. It didn't take long to find out how much you could buy with a pack of smokes. Everything was priced in cigarettes on the black market. Cash was worth five to one, sometimes more.

One day, having been here about eight months, I was reading in the law library that I could appeal my conviction, and get out of here on what was called an appeal bond. What I had to do was contact my lawyer and tell him that I wanted to appeal my conviction, and then the state Supreme Court would have to set a bond. All I needed was ten percent of the amount and I would walk. My mind went to work with this thought. I started writing letters to my friends on the outside, and before long I had the bail money. In less than a month I was out of prison. I knew that my appeal had no hope of being overturned and my lawyer told me so. I did, after all, plead guilty but I would get a break from here and come back and finish the sentence when it was more convenient. So, as I was walking toward the gate for release, all my partners were there yelling, "Don't forget us man… send us some money… send some pictures of babes… find some girls that will write to us."

I hadn't been out on bond but three weeks when I bumped into Earl. He was a man that had been a volunteer counselor at the community corrections center I was in before going to prison. We used to get along pretty well and from time to time we smoked some bud together. So we talked for a couple of hours and then we agreed to meet again the next day to talk over a possible job idea he had. He told me that he had been thinking for some time that I would be the guy for the task, and was glad he ran in to me. He had heard that I went to prison and wasn't surprised at all that I had found a way out. I thought this to be interesting that one of my former counselors would want to discuss doing a job together.

Well, lunch was over and we were driving a rental car, headed out of state to run a game. I was really excited about the prospect so I kept running the ideas of how to do it thru my mind. It would require me to make a call and share some pertinent information with the person that answered the telephone. So I rehearsed the lines over and over for two days. I knew what I would say and exactly how I would say it. Sitting at a pay phone I dialed the number. I told him that I knew what he had been up to and that there were those who would be greatly disappointed in him if they found out. I said that calling the FBI wasn't a good idea because I had copied the information and it would be delivered to his boss if something happened to me. All he could say was, "How did you find out?"

We set up the drop for later that night. I parked in a position where I could watch him all day through the window where he worked. I never let him out of my sight. At one point I stood beside him in the checkout line in the drug store. My heart was pounding all afternoon watching the guy. He must have been wondering where I had gotten my information, and I'm sure that the question haunted him all afternoon. He had never met me and had no idea who I was as I sat at the table across from him when he ate his lunch at Denny's.

It went like clockwork. He left work and went to the bank. He was in there no more than ten minutes and walked out and drove off to the drop spot. He did exactly as he was instructed to and then drove away. I watched from a distance as he turned on to the freeway. We waited in a bar across the street shooting pool from a place that we could watch the money. We watched for hours, making sure he didn't return and that no cops showed up. Then, while Earl drove the car, I went and picked up the bag of money. We had done it. We were now on the freeway headed out of town. I was remembering how I saw a similar con played on television in some spy movie. *Yes,* I thought, *I liked the action.* It was better than drugs. I felt alive and prison was no longer on my mind.

Chapter 26

A Flight to Texas

We had made a clean get away and were driving toward Minneapolis. I now wanted to put some distance between Earl and me. So I told him to drop me off at a hotel along the freeway and he could return the rental car when he got back to town. I told him that we would talk in a few days. So, standing outside the hotel, I waited for him to drive off and then I went in and called a cab. I wanted more distance between us, and I didn't want Earl to know where I was, or where I was going to be staying. You never know when someone is going to roll over on you. They don't need a reason. They simply do it. I thought for a moment that this guy was one of my counselors less than a year ago. Who knows what is going on in his head now?

I got out of the cab and went into the airport terminal, and purchased a one-way ticket to Corpus Christi, Texas. The flight would leave early in the morning, so I got another cab and went to a different hotel and checked in for the night. I used the name Phillip Walker, paid cash, and ordered a four-thirty a.m. wake up call. Then I went to my room and fell into a deep sleep.

I have always enjoyed flying, and stepping off the plane, I decided that I liked Texas too. I rented a new

Ford LTD and started driving until I found a hotel that looked acceptable for me to cool off for a month or so. The bellman showed me to the room and it suited me well. It was a suite with a large living room and the bedroom was toward the back. I had a private balcony overlooking the pool and I could see the front desk from here too. I had paid the rent for a month in advance, so this would help me from having to spend much time in the lobby. Now it was time to put everything behind me and plan for a life in Mexico. Sitting by the pool, it felt great being here and no one knowing where I was. I kind of liked the sound of my current name Stewart Thomas. Yes, I liked it.

Minnesota, Iowa, and prison seemed so far away now. They were behind me, like the other places with bad memories I wanted to forget, like Georgetown and all the hell on Church Street. Now, as I was sitting here, my entire life was passing through my mind at a rapid pace like a silent movie on fast-forward. It had been fifteen years now since my mother had been killed, and only seven years since living in Florida. What I was seeing of myself now, in my thoughts, was not looking good. Where would I end up in life? There was still the fact of being out of prison on bond, and what if Earl opened his mouth about the little caper we pulled. *Oh well,* I thought, *no one got hurt*. It wasn't like we robbed someone. And besides that, the guy shouldn't have let anyone know what he what he done. So he had to pay up some money. He had plenty of it. He wasn't complaining, and I wouldn't ever say anything. He didn't even know who I was. Only that I existed. That was enough.

Oh yes, my life was missing something, and I didn't know what it was. I had some cash to get me through for a long time, women were sitting around the pool in their swimming suits, the tequila was good and I was smoking some sweet bud. Yet it seemed that the world was closing in on me. I felt it more than knew it. What would become of me was my thought. This was fun, sure, but it wasn't what I wanted. I was disappointed in myself and all alone. The dreams I had as a boy were full of action and excitement, but jail had never been a consideration. It sure was now.

It was time to make a call and find out what was going on back in the mid-west. I had always given someone a little misinformation. That way I could gauge the situation by what they were telling me. I was talking to my friend over the telephone and it seemed that Earl, sometime after dropping me off, had been in a car accident and ended up in the hospital. He had a broken collarbone, one of his arms was in a cast, and a shoulder and his left leg were broken too. He had totaled the car and was in a coma for three days before coming out of it. According to my friend, while in the emergency room, they gave Earl some Sodium Pentothal for the pain, and he was talking and saying, "Chuck we should have never done it," and words like that. Now the feds were interested in talking to me. That's all I needed. So giving this a couple of days thought, I decided to hop in my rental car and drive back to St. Paul.

I hadn't seen or talked to Foster in a few years so I gave him a call and he invited me to stay with him while I was in town. We had first met while I lived in the apartment building in St. Paul with my dad. I knew his sisters and his mother and so it didn't take long for us to be friends. I even dated his niece for a while back in the day. His family referred to us as the salt and pepper team. It had to do with the difference in the color of our skin, him being black and me being white and all. I remember his mother once telling me that if we were in New Orleans I would get myself killed for dating a black girl and running with Foster. She said that it wouldn't be a black person either, that it would be my own kind. We had been partners and friends for a long while and now. I was looking forward to seeing him, and I had missed St. Paul and was glad to be back.

A few nights later we went out on the town with a couple friends. We went to all the places we use to go to. The night started off really good. We were shooting pool at a club and winning some money when club security came and told us that we had to leave. Their excuse was Foster's shirt. Seemed that it didn't meet the dress code. Right. We were winning everyone's money. We knew the real reason. It was what we called the skin game. Oh well, we had both been here before. As we left, I shared with him the time in New Mexico when I was given plastic ware and a paper plate to eat on in a restaurant, while everyone else had melmac plates and silverware. I was the only white person in the place. I felt uncomfortable at the time, but I wasn't leaving until I ate my dinner.

So with Foster driving the car and me in the passenger seat twisting up a joint and laying out a couple of lines of blow, we drove down the strip a few times so all his friends could see him driving a new Ford LTD. With the tape player turned up, playing some James Brown, we were jamming and having a good time, and all my troubles seemed to fade away.

We parked the car and walked to the door of the club. I had been here many times before with Foster. We had played pool and spent many of our afternoons at the Metropolitan Club, drinking and partying. As we rang the bell on the door, three big men answered and talking to Foster they said, "You and the ladies are welcome to come on in, but," and they rolled their eyes toward me and said, "he has to go." Foster told them that I was alright and that I had been here many times before, but they didn't give in so we left. Foster was not happy at all about this and was apologizing to me for the way I had been treated by his friends. This was twice tonight that we had both experienced discrimination. We were proud of our friendship, knowing that we had broken the skin game barrier. So, shaking our heads, we got into the car and went to pick up our dates for the evening.

We had been partying and dancing all night having a great time, and then we decided to get some food and call it a night. It was already early in the morning so we pulled in to a burger joint before going back to the house. We had made the best of all that had taken place earlier in the evening, so after we had some food we were going to take the ladies home and sleep all day. As we stood in line waiting for our order to come, two men started saying some things about us being mixed couples and how we should keep to our own kind. I didn't pay too much attention to what they were saying. I figured they had been drinking. However, Foster had had enough of what had gone on already in the night, and now here again. I paid for our food and Foster had already gone to the car and was, I thought, waiting for us. All of a sudden he came out from the front seat of the car and started shooting his pistol at the two men who had walked out behind him. I ducked for cover with the women as not to get shot. By this time he had emptied the clip and was reloading when the security guard drew down on him and yelled freeze. Then he cuffed him and held him until the heat got there. I motioned for the women to get in the car and we drove away.

Chapter 27

California Run

I was in Fargo, North Dakota when I called to see what had happened to Foster. His mother told me that he was still in jail and would be there at least until he went to court. I asked her to give him a message for me and hung up and got back in the car. I couldn't wait around with the heat I had on me, so getting out of town was a wise move.

I had only met Kathy a few days ago and here we were heading to California together. She wasn't saying too much about herself and I didn't ask. I sure wasn't telling her what kind of mess I was in. We both seemed to prefer it that way. And about the shooting two nights ago, we didn't talk much about that at all. Somewhere in Montana we spotted two guys on the side of the road so I stopped and picked them up. They were hitchhiking to California. They told us that they had recently graduated from high school and were making that California trip of their dreams. Funny, I thought, how young they seemed to be, and then it dawned on me that I had made that trip twice myself and I was only twenty-three. We were all talking and having a fun time. I was sure that they didn't quite know what to think about us. We were driving a brand new car, smoking all the bud we wanted and had the appearance of having money. To top it off neither one of them could keep from staring at Kathy. She was a knock out blonde and she knew it, so she played in to the game of their watching and staring at her. I thought it was funny. These guys would sure have a story to tell some day about their trip with us.

The northern California sea breeze felt good blowing in my face as I was standing on the beach looking out into the ocean. It reminded me of the rides in my dad's truck when the wind was blowing through my hair. I hadn't thought about my troubles now for a few days, but inside I was feeling the effects, and it seemed to me that I was having conversations with myself. This was something that used to happen to me way back in Georgetown too. It was like I was in a battle inside my mind with myself. How weird. I thought that it was almost real. I was having these thoughts more and more lately and they were pounding in my head, giving me migraines.

Kathy was acting like she was my girl, always hanging on me, laying her head on my shoulder or holding my hand. I wasn't sure if she was for real or if perhaps she was doing it for the boys' benefit, the way she moved when she walked and seemed to look their way. And she was on my mind more than I wanted her to be. I mean, I thought she was Foster's girl. I made it to the coast like we had planned, but wasn't too sure what to do next. The hitchhikers didn't seem to want the fun they were having with us to end. I think that they were surprised when I said, "Why don't you guys go down the beach and hang out with Kathy?" They both looked at me and at each other and headed in her direction. It was funny I thought, they had the same puppy love expressions on their faces that I must have had a few years ago sitting in Mrs. Ross's English classroom. She was the most beautiful woman I had ever seen and I was sure she knew that I thought so too.

Back on the freeway I was driving fast and trying to keep up with the southern California drivers when I saw a highway patrol car come up behind me. I was speeding with everyone else and didn't want to look suspicious by slowing down so I kept going with the traffic. I switched lanes causally wanting to exit and he did too. He stayed behind me for some time and then looking in the rear view mirror I saw that he had turned on his lights. I was being pulled over. I had a dozen thoughts going on in my head as I came to a stop, and the feeling in my gut was all too familiar. The next thing I knew the cop was standing at my window asking me if I knew why I had been pulled over.

"No sir," I replied. I handed him the driver's license I had and he walked back to the squad car.

I was sure the boys didn't know what to think about this, but I did, oh yes. I had been here before and I knew it go one of two ways. If my ID passed, I would be alright. If it didn't, I was going to jail. Looking behind me another cop car pulled up. This wasn't good I thought, so I told the guys in the back to sit still, and do whatever the cops tell them if they wanted to get out of this. Then cops with shotguns surrounded us. They ordered me out of the car and onto the ground. Holding a gun on me, another cop handcuffed me and said that I was under arrest. Kathy was in handcuffs too. I still didn't know if it was the bank job or for something else. I told the police that the boys were hitchhikers and so they treated them really well. Seeing the look on their faces as we were lying on the side of the road, I knew they would have some story to tell about this ride.

Sitting in my cell back in the reformatory I was thinking about how lucky I had been in California. If I had only called the car rental company in Texas and extended my rental time, I would never have been picked up in California. Well, I couldn't blame them. They wanted to know where their car was, so they reported it stolen. If I would have thought a little clearer, I would properly be in Mexico living it up now, but instead, I served ninety days in the L.A. county jail on federal interstate theft and got five years probation. There was a letter from my lawyer waiting for me at my dad's house when I got back from the coast. The letter stated that my appeal case had no merit. *Really,* I thought. Well I had a good vacation while it lasted. So I checked myself in prison to get it out of the way.

The reformatory wasn't all that bad a place and besides I was going to be out in another ten months anyway. I was working in the furniture shop and had a pretty good job. The foreman was a nice man and we got along real well. Seemed that he was some kind of a minister on Sundays too. We shared an interest in honeybees and so we spent hours talking about them. I really liked the guy and some of the stories he would share. He talked about God some and made references to the bible from time to time. He reminded me of my Grandfather when he would tell me stories about God and Jesus and all of that stuff. Some of the other guys in the shop were rude to him and didn't like what he was talking about. I felt bad for the way they seemed to ridicule him. He was a champ however. If it bothered him at all it never showed.

Kathy was writing to me regularly and keeping me up to speed with what was happening back in Minnesota. We had become friends on our adventure together and it was nice getting mail from her. Today when I opened her letter she had written that Foster had been shot in the head at a bar. She wrote that he had stepped in to a fight between two friends to help when one of them pulled a pistol and shot him six times. This was sad and heart breaking news. My friend was shot and may not make it. Bad news in prison is always received hard, mainly because there is nothing you can do about it, except think, and ponder and end up feeling sorry for yourself.

As I was riding the Greyhound bus toward home I was reflecting over the past few years of my life. That conversation was going on in my head again, bouncing back and forth. I was having those thoughts again that were not my own and I tried to get them out of my mind. I was glad for one thing however. The parole board let me out of prison and I was looking forward to making a clean start when I got back home to Minnesota. I had a job lined up so I was thinking about buying a trailer house to get started, and laying low for a while. One thing I wasn't looking forward to was the meeting with my parole officer. She and I had met before when I was on probation for the scam with Dad and Susan. So I closed my eyes and tried to get some sleep but was having thoughts about my mother. I wanted to cry.

Chapter 28

Helen and A Bat out of Hell

John was in the halfway house with me before I went to prison, and now we were sitting around talking about old times. I was dating his younger sister before I went to Iowa to do the safe job with Poppy, and I asked how she was doing since I hadn't seen her in some time. He told me that she had gotten married and her husband was a nice man and they were doing well together. I asked him about everyone else and how people were doing, and he said that his other sister had gotten a divorce from her husband. This was sad I thought, because they seemed to be so happy and I used to spend some weekends there when I dated John's sister.

The trailer was a nice one for the money and so I purchased it, cleaned it up, and began furnishing it. With Dad and Susan's help, we had it looking good with fresh paint and drapes. It was located a few minute's drive from the gas station where I worked part time.

I was doing well and things were going real smooth for me. My brother came down with some of his friends and his very needy girlfriend, and we had a house warming party. The trailer was full of people and the music playing some old tunes on the radio. *Yes,* I thought, things were going good for me and prison was a long way from my thoughts. My home was feeling comfortable and I had some money saved. I was feeling good with how far I had come. Even with how well I was doing I continued to have the conversations in my mind and I couldn't seem to shake them. Even after all the years I would think about my mother and wonder how my life would have turned out had she been alive.

I was sitting home one night watching some TV and thought I would give Helen a call and see if what she was doing. So I called and asked if she wanted to get together to talk about old times and go out or something. She accepted and that weekend we went out, and caught up on some old times. She seemed to want to talk about when I dated her sister, and asked me if I remembered this or that, and if I thought her sister was prettier than she was, and that kind of stuff. We went out to dinner and then to see a movie and then I drove her home that evening and didn't talk to her again for about a month.

Then one day she and a friend of hers showed up at my trailer. She wanted to know what I would think about her becoming my roommate and moving in with me. I asked what she meant by "my roommate," and so we had an agreement and she moved in with me the next week. She was a little homemaker and put some of her touches on the trailer making it real homey. I would come home for lunch hour from work every night and have supper, and then she would be waiting up for me when I got home at the end of my shift. We would smoke some weed, drink a little wine, and listen to Meat Loaf's album "Bat out of Hell" every night. We had all the songs memorized by heart.

One weekend we decided to take a road trip to Illinois and get married. We had let some people know what we were doing to do, and they had a party planned for when we got back home. The problem was that we had a fight during the trip, called the marriage off, and headed home. The not getting married didn't bother me so much, but I had driven hundreds of miles in a snowstorm with a woman that I could have just as easily busted upside the head. The mouth and the nagging, I couldn't believe what I was seeing and hearing. What a turn in events! It was almost like she was expecting to get slapped in the face or something. I had thought of leaving her and her mouth at a truck stop and driving off, but I felt sorry for her the way she was behaving. All she did was sit there, staring out the window, staring into space. And then I realized that she was a hurting and troubled woman inside, and I began to feel sorry for her. I was always doing that it seemed, feeling sorry for someone that had a hard life. Seemed that I could relate well to what it was like to be hurt and abused by others. One thing I had learned was to get over it, put it in check.

We hadn't been home ten minutes when the telephone rang, and we were being congratulated for getting married. I had barely hung up the receiver and there was a knock at the door, people were flooding into the house. The party was still on. Standing there looking at each other we didn't say a word about the fact we didn't get married. We let everyone think we were, as not to let them down. And so the masquerade went on until that June when we finely stood before the judge and tied the knot.

The following October our daughter was born to us and we were happy to welcome her in to the world. She was a cutie pie and I couldn't get enough of holding her. It had been a close call that day, as I rushed her mother to the hospital blowing the horn and driving through red lights to get there. She was born fifteen minutes later. The day we brought her home was a really happy day for me and it seemed that things had finally worked themselves out. I would spend hours holding my little girl, kissing her and loving her. And now we had turned a chapter in our lives and we had plans of moving in to a new house in the spring.

Chapter 29

Under Arrest

We really liked our little house but we didn't seem to get along unless we were smoking weed or if we had people over. I was still having the thoughts in my head and the battle would rage some days for hours. And now there were the added thoughts of where I was in my life and living with a wife I couldn't stand. Her mouth was always running, talking smack and wanting to engage me in a fight. To complicate things even more was that now we had a child to be concerned for. I was asking myself why I had married her and was feeling like I did it more because I felt sorry for her than I loved her. What a mess I was in I thought and then when I had enough I slapped her up side the head. That didn't seem to accomplish anything. She would keep on running her mouth.

I had spent the afternoon with my buddy in the back room of his liquor store reloading pistol shells. Rich had a good little set up going. He sold booze up front and guns in the back. Funny thing that the same Federal office was in charge of both. So not only did he have a license to sell liquor, he had to have a Federal firearms license too. I would joke and kid him about how much he had the man in his business. We had no love for the BATF because all they wanted was to take away our guns, and with the Contras losing in San

Salvador it wouldn't be long until we would need to defend our homes from the Communists. If they came, we were ready. We had been buying guns and ammo for years. Not only that, but we had gas masks, ammo, clothing, food and water stored up for a few years. One thing we made sure of was that we shot the same type bullets. I, of course, had my forty-five autos for short-up close range loaded with hollow points. And everyone needed a 12-gauge twelve-seventy for short range loaded with double-aught buckshot. Of course I had to have a .223 mini fourteen too.

Rich had been to a gun show the past weekend and picked up some British practice ammo with the hopes of being able to shoot and reload them. The Brits used these shells on the practice range and once they were fired, threw them away. These shells had three flash holes instead of the standard one, so with a punch and a rifle primer we seemed to be in luck. I would take some home and test fire them tonight. He had purchased a few thousand rounds, so we would have more shells to add to the supply.

I had been home long enough to say hello, hold my daughter for a while, have a sandwich and wash it down with a cup of coffee. I got my forty-five out, slid it into my waistband, and with some shells in my pocket went outside to do some target practice. I walked about fifty feet and placed a target in the firing range. As I turned to walk back to the shooting area, I noticed something out of place. I could see some activity that caught my eye, so I started for the house keeping my attention on what was going on up the road. It looked as though the cops were about to do a bust on the tavern. I could see them pulling into position. From my vantage point there must have been thirty of them. Something big was about to go down, so I thought I would get in the car and drive by and, if possible, warn the people in the tavern of what was about to happen. I ducked into the house and took my gun off and put it away and emptied my pockets of shells. Then I picked up my car keys and went outside.

My house sat about sixty yards off the highway and there were railroad tracks between the road and me. So I got into my car, pulled up out of the driveway and turned left toward the highway when all of a sudden there were cops coming out from everywhere. From behind bushes, in cars, with lights flashing. They blocked me in with cars and surrounded me with guns pulled and all pointed at me. *What the hell was going on?* I thought as I stopped the car.

One guy at the passenger's window had a shotgun pointed at me yelling, "Get out of the car!"

There was another cop walking up from behind me on the left side with his handgun pointed at me. I watched him from my mirror and then he started yelling "Get out of the car, hands up! Don't move! Out of the car, now! Show me your hands, show me your hands"

I had my foot on the brake. I wasn't moving it. My hands were in the air, but the car was still in drive and I didn't dare move a hand to put it into park or move my foot off the brake. *Stay cool,* I thought, *wait, and don't move.*

When a cop could see my face I told him that the car was in gear.

"Out of the car, @#*&^."

"The car is in gear!" I yelled back.

Then another cop opened the passenger side door and reached in to turn off the engine while the guy that was on my left side pointed a shotgun at me. "Don't move or I'll blow your head off," he yelled.

As soon as the car was turned off they dragged me out and threw me to the ground. Four or five officers jumped on top of me. One had his pistol against my ear. "Don't move! You're under arrest. Where are the guns? Where are your *&%$# guns? Where are your automatic weapons?"

They picked me up, searched me and threw me into the back of the police car. As the police car moved toward the highway I looked back and saw my little daughter in the arms of her mother crying for her daddy.

I lay awake staring at the ceiling. I hated the place I had gotten myself into it again. All my dreams and plans down the drain. My new home would be lost. My little daughter. I felt so bad for her, thinking of how she cried when they drove off with me in the police car. I hoped that she would be taken care of well and that I would see her soon. My dad and his wife, they wouldn't bail me out of this one, even if I could get bail, and I doubted that. My parole officer, she was a piece of work anyway, had had her fill of me. No way she was letting me out of jail. I was here and for the long haul. I fell off to sleep feeling sorry for myself and wishing I were anyplace but here.

The cops kept me in a cell by myself for three weeks and that was getting old real quick. I had asked to be moved, but the answer was always the same, "Wait and see."

I had been here long enough to know what that meant. Same old, same old. Say one thing and do another. Jail guards were cops that couldn't make it, so they got stuck here, and they thought they were something. I had met plenty of them. Big men at work and when they go home they slap around the old lady and the kids. And then there was the guy down the hall in another cell, yelling all day long, pounding on his walls. I was hoping to deal with him later. Yes, things never seem to change in jail. Games and more games. The cops had theirs and so did the inmates. I hated it and yet found myself right smack back in the middle of it. I had no one to blame for my situation except myself, and I think that was the reality that hurt the most. This was my mess and no one else's but mine!

Finally, they moved me into a cellblock with some other inmates. At least I could play some cards and have room to walk around. I could stand on the bars and see the street from my cell. How I would love to be out there I thought. Being alone in a cell had its benefits. There was no one around to hear you cry and weep as you bury your face into a pillow.

A few days later, late in the middle of the night, they brought in three new inmates and put them in our cellblock. They were up all night long shuffling and banging decks of cards on the steel tables. I rolled over twice and asked them to keep the noise down. Then a little later they were wrestling and horse playing. I was ticked, but thought I would wait until morning to deal with these three punks. So I tried to get to sleep but the battle was going on in my head and had been for days now. All night long I lay in the bunk thinking how I was going to deal with these three guys.

As soon as breakfast was served I walked over to the table and said, "Which of you punks kept me awake all night?" No one answered.

So I said it one more time and no one answered. So I busted one of them up side the head and took his breakfast and walked over to the other two sissies and took theirs too. Then I told them that they were evicted and to get out of my cellblock and to get out now. They ran over to the door, knocking for the guard. The guard came to the door and asked them what all the noise was about and what it was that they wanted. They said that they were kicked out of the cellblock and that they needed to move now. I thought that it was great what they were told by the guard, "You boys stay in there with Chuck and don't bother me anymore."

The trial had lasted four days and cost me all of my money for my attorney's fees and now here I'm sitting in a cell four months since being arrested waiting for the jury to come back with a not guilty verdict. I wanted it to be over. I had been here long enough. I hated jail and everything about it. The dream I had the night before kept on going through in my mind.

My dad and the guys would come crashing through the gates and break me out. I would make my escape across the Mississippi river and jump a freight train south, head down to Central America and join up with the Contras. And then reality hit home. My dad had never been there for me. Never. Not once.

My lawyer told me earlier in the day that the longer the jury was out the better my chances were of getting found not guilty. It was now nearly ten at night and I was feeling pretty sure of myself. I had asked the jailer if they had heard anything and he told me that the jury was still deliberating. *Good,* I thought to myself. I was going home. I beat the case and I would be out of here soon. I had no longer had the thought when the guard came back to my cell to get me.

"The jury is back with a verdict," he said.
I was led to the courtroom at eleven-thirty at night to stand in front of the judge to hear my fate. As I stood there with my lawyer listening to the judge ask the jury if they had reached a verdict my hope was running high.

Then the jury foreman said, "Yes, your honor. We find the defendant guilty as charged."

Chapter 30

The State Prison

The walk up the long steps was the hardest and longest walk of my life. I was handcuffed with my hands behind my back, and they were digging into my wrist, and I had shackles around my ankles. I was walking toward the front gate of the state prison with a guard holding my arm. The place looked like a castle out of some movie. It was built out of granite stone, gray and cold looking, with large iron bars. This was going to be my home for the next three years I thought, as the sound of the iron gate slammed behind me, completely shutting me off from the outside world. Now here I was once again inside another prison. The fear of the unknown started to settle into my already tight gut. And the voices in my mind were screaming, laughing, and ridiculing me.

Inside, I had dozens of thoughts going on in my mind all at the same time. *Look straight ahead. Don't look at anyone in the eye. Walk tall. Don't look scared and don't look weak.* I asked myself what all the big deal was. I'd been in prison before. *Buck up.* I was standing in the middle of the turnkey with heavy thick glass all around me. There was the door behind me that led to freedom and then the door before me that led to the inside of the prison. Behind the glass were guards looking over my papers. Even at this point, standing here, I held on to hope that this was as far as I would have to go. Somehow there had been a mistake made. Why couldn't I have my guns? So what if I had been a convicted felon?

With that thought still fresh in my mind, the gate opened and I was greeted by two guards that, from the looks of them, would rather have been somewhere else today as well. They led me to the new inmate receiving area and began processing me in to the institution. I hated the looks of the place, the smell and the sounds. Everything was loud and noisy. I was in a vacuum with my emotion and thoughts, trying to remain calm. Then with the processing finished I was given some clothes, a new pair of state made shoes, some toiletry stuff, two towels and a set of sheets that I could see thru. Then I was led down a long hallway to the cellblock.

The cellblock was a big loud place that housed three hundred plus men. I walked past cell after cell down to the end, then up two flights of stairs until I was in front of my cell. The door was opened and I was told to go inside and then the door closed behind me. As the guard was leaving I asked him, "What's next?"

He said, "Next? There is no next, make yourself at home."

The cell was filthy dirty. The sink and toilet were plugged and the floor had not been cleaned in awhile either. I was glad to have a broom and cleaning supplies already in the cell, so I went about cleaning my house. As I finished up my cleaning and made the bed a porter came to bring me a sack lunch for my evening meal as I had arrived too late for chow that evening. Somehow I was glad that I didn't have to leave my cell. When the lights went out for the night, the place got very quiet and still. I wondered as I lay there, alone in my thoughts, if this is what others were doing also. I was weeping inside as I buried my face into the pillow so no one would hear me. My eyes were wet with tears and my nose needed blowing again. I was so far away from anyone I knew. There would be no phone calls tonight, no one coming over to the house. No, I was here on my own, by my doing and no one else's, and as I started to fall asleep I recalled the words of grandmother so long ago, "You make your own bed, now sleep in it."

The time was going by much faster than I would have imagined. I had been here six months and had gotten about as comfortable as one could get while locked up. I mean, I had a television, a stereo and was cooking food in my house using the coffee pot when I didn't want to go to the dining hall to eat their slop. Yes, I'd say I was doing alright. I had a sweet little job working in the tractor shop and after breakfast this morning the boys and me were going to spend the day tripping on some blotter acid. So I locked my cell door with a padlock and was walking to breakfast with my partners when some guy walked up beside me and called me a punk snitch. I recognized him as a guy from a halfway house I'd been in, so didn't give it much thought. He had been a sissy there and no doubt he was here too. I had once before punched him in the face for running his mouth on me. Maybe he needed some more. After chow I headed back for the cell hall when someone from our group came up and told me, "You have to try and kill that punk that called you a snitch or move out of the cell next to mine. You can't even walk with us until you kill that punk"

I knew that this was now a problem and I had better take care of it, now, today. Being called a punk and not doing anything about it meant that you could become a victim yourself real fast. *Well, I wasn't any punk,* I thought, *and so I'll have to do what I have to do.*

Standing in my cell waiting for morning count to be over, I thought how only two hours ago I was doing okay. Now I have to kill a man for running his mouth on me. Inside, my guts were tight and I didn't like the situation I was in. Pounding this punk wasn't a problem. After all I had punched out my share of big mouths. Somehow they always mistake my kindness for weakness, and then when I let loose on them for crossing the line, it is always somehow my fault. Well, he was a punk and I really never did like him anyway, recalling the group meetings back at the program, and their two rules. No violence and no threats of violence. I even thought that this was why these guys could get away with running their mouths. They always had the group leader or the man protecting them. The more I thought about it the more I wanted to bust this punk's head. The thing was to do it and don't get caught. I had decided that I wouldn't kill him. If I wanted to kill someone there were others ahead of him on my list. But he did have something coming and if I didn't do it good enough I could be next.

As the buzzer sounded I moved quickly to get into position to take care of business, careful not to appear like I was making a move. I walked out into the main flow of people and waited a bit. Then I saw him on the other side of the hall, just passing me and looking like he was some kind of bad &%#. So I moved a little faster and got up beside him. As he turned to see me, I let a punch fly and nailed him squarely in the nose as hard as I could. Then I went down on top of him as he fell down to the ground, and pounded his face in to the floor two or three times. I was up and on my feet, back into the flow of people before the guards even made it over to where he was laying. He was bleeding all over himself and crying like the punk sissy he was as a guard helped him to his feet. I thought to myself, *You punk. Run your mouth on me. How does it feel now, big mouth? You better call your momma,* and I continued to my job assignment feeling good. Yes, that helped me take the edge off, got it out of my system. Punk!

I had been locked up a year now with no more problems with the man or the cons. I had learned my way around pretty well and was now working in the commissary and canteen, one of the most coveted jobs in the joint, and I loved it. One day I thought to myself that there was a great opportunity knocking here, and what I needed was a plan. In prison the currency was anything of value. Cash money was worth five or ten to one. On the other hand cigarettes, coffee, and stamped envelopes were a real commodity. People used them to trade with, and I worked in the Fort Knox of the prison. There was case after case of cigarettes and coffee stacked up to the ceiling. Now all I had to do was figure out how to get my hands on some of it. That evening I talked to someone that could put me in touch with the trash crew. Yes! I had a plan and needed a partner.

I had my feet up on the desk in my cell watching some TV and smoking a joint when someone walked by cell and said to look over the railing, someone wanted to talk with me. I thought about it for a moment before looking, and when I did there sat my soon to be partner, Chief Lacy. He was a big, tall, ugly looking dude that had been here for many years. The Chief motioned with his eyes for me to come down and so I went to have our first meeting. On the way I thought, *this is one scary looking dude.* I had heard about him before, and the talk was that he was one of the most feared and respected men by the cons in the institution. It didn't take long before me and the chief were doing business and I had to admit to myself I liked the dude. When the chief walked down the hallway people seemed to move out of his way. Many people feared this man.

Twice a week when the trash was set out from the canteen, some of the bags contained the loot and Chief would take it from there. While the guard drove the trash truck to the next stop chief would find the stash and hide it until the end of the day. Then he would bring it into the cell hall. We had so many cartons of smokes that we had to have other people keep them in their cells for us. The same with coffee and envelopes. A month or so later we worked out a deal with a guy that ran a two for one store on the lower galley.

The store man sold anything you wanted, and he cooked the best fried ham and cheese sandwich in the joint. He cooked on an iron he ripped off from the laundry and the ham and cheese arrived in laundry carts to the cellblock from the kitchen. Oh yes, I was a player now. I had found some action. This place wasn't so bad, not like I had heard. Heck, I was doing all right. I didn't run with a gang like many of the men did. I had always depended on myself, and there was no one I trusted.

Working in the canteen had its other advantages as well. On pay days the line to buy stuff from the canteen was long, and people would have to stand and wait some times for hours to get through to spend their monthly pay. I knew who the leaders of the gangs were, and so they never had to stand in line and wait. As soon as I saw them enter the area, I pushed their order slip forward and in and out they went. I was playing every angle I could and the favors were paid in kind. I always had dope to smoke.

One day someone came to my cell and told me that Michael Cain wanted to see me. This guy was the mayor of the joint. He was the top dog and the leader of the biggest gang. He could order something and it was finished. This man could call a strike, he could call a riot, and you could be killed if he said so. Now here I was standing outside his cell for what I didn't know, but he wanted to see me and that's all I needed to hear. When he saw me I was told to come into his house and there was another guy there too. He looked at the other guy, a member of his group, and asked him, "Is this the guy?"

And he said, "Yes."

And then he told the other, "This is my canteen man. Don't ever look at him again or come to me with a problem concerning him."

Wow, I thought to myself, *what was this about?* Seemed that I had said something to this guy that he didn't like when he was in the canteen line, so he went and thought he was going to use some weight on me. *Oh well,* I thought as I went back to my house, *I'm doing all right.*

I was almost two years inside, and Christmas was coming up soon. I had been divorced now three months, and hadn't seen my little daughter one time. Seemed to me that the judge would enforce the visiting order, but then I really didn't expect it. I couldn't blame her if she didn't want to come up here to see me, but then, yes, I could. The judge did order her to bring my baby girl to see me once a month, and I hadn't seen her yet. *You &%$#@,* I thought, and the anger would build and build as I started to hate her. She didn't answer of my letters, was never home when I called, and no one knew where she was. The thoughts of my ex-wife enraged me. I was tossed back and forth with caring for someone and hating them at the same time. The more I thought about her the more I loathed her. I had thoughts of how to knock her off, where to do it, how to get away with it. Week after week I tried to make contact. I wrote letters, called people, and they hadn't seen her. I tried a prayer one night. That didn't work either. Finally, with a splitting headache, I went to sleep hoping that the battle in my mind would stop.

I began to spend more time than usual in my cell, off into my thoughts, partly feeling self-pity and partly disapproving of everyone I knew. My dad and his wife didn't write or come to visit, didn't bring my daughter to see me but once, and then complained about the money he had to spend on gas for the drive up here. He was most likely still remembering the day at the gas station three years ago. I told him then if he made one step toward me the way he was acting and screaming at me, that I would knock his &^%$ head off. I was sure he finally got the message, knowing that I was more than able to get the job done. I mean, after all, who did he think he was yelling at the way he did in front of my wife? I should have beat the *&^%$ out of him that day. He had it coming and he knew it. I finally saw him scared that day, and even better than that, he knew it. I wasn't the little kid anymore that he could beat and push around that day. And here I was sitting in a prison cell, calling it my house, and thinking that I was something. Then the truth, the stark reality set in. I wasn't anything more than what I did on the outside, and getting nowhere in life.

New Year's Eve was coming up and the hooch I had cooking in my footlocker was starting to smell real good. I sure hoped the plastic bags would hold up, and more than that, that the man wouldn't smell it or find it in a shake down. We were going to party hardy, and get blasted on my raisin jack. The mule had come through and we had a big sack of weed and some acid, oh yes. So I locked my house and headed for the canteen to work. It was a slow day so we played spades, smoked some bud and zoned out. I was about to deal another hand of cards when a guard told me to report to the captain's office in the security center. Walking down the hall I had a tight knot in my gut thinking that my brew was smelling pretty strong. As I entered the security center, sure enough there was my footlocker. Busted. Thirty days in solitary confinement.

Prison. Oh well. You can make the best of a bad situation, but solitary confinement is ugly. There is no TV, no smokes, and no dope. I mean there is nothing except sleep, eat, and sleep and one shower a week. I was having no fun at all. I was cold, didn't have enough to eat, and missed my cell with all the comforts of home. I was beginning to hate prison even more. I lay awake at night thinking about my life and the mess I had made of myself. And then I would sleep all day long. I was having dreams about the outside. Bad thing to think about the streets. It will drive you crazy thinking about the outside while in prison. I was having more and more dreams. Hating those who had let me down. My dad and his wife, some piece of work they were. I took the heat for them a few years ago and that cost me some county time. And my ex-wife - who knows where she had gotten to. She could have crawled in a hole and died as far as I knew. Where is my daughter? That was the big question I wanted answered. I missed her so much. I had to get out of here. There has to be a way. I'll find one, some how. Maybe treatment? Treatment... What a stupid idea. There is a program in the State Reformatory I thought, but treatment? Sitting in a group with all those punks yelling at me. Yah right. I have gone that route before. Well maybe it would be worth a look. No.

Chapter 31

Treatment 1983 and 1984

"You have to change! You have an image problem. If you don't stop and take a look at what people are telling you, you will end up right back here in prison. You won't be on the streets a month!" The group had been yelling and screaming at me for over an hour now.

"Take a look at yourself! What makes you think you have changed? You like prison." The group goal was to break down my defenses so I would stop and look at myself, and change my way of doing things.

I yelled back at all of them, "Shut up punk! Who you think you're yelling at? Who are you to tell me anything? You're in prison too, stupid!"

And then I laughed at them. This would only bring on more. They yelled and screamed at me for days and weeks on end. They really cared about me. This was part of what went on in this type of intense group therapy. I didn't feel like crying in front of these people, and if they thought that some screaming at me was going to shake me up they were wrong. I wasn't some weak punk and yet, I wanted to change my life.

I was in the treatment program at the state reformatory and I had been here for two weeks. This was a live in community within the prison, where I would spend twelve hours a day sitting in lectures, learning Transactional Analysis. I found that I really enjoyed the teaching and that I could relate to and understand what I was being taught. The treatment information was based on the theories of Eric Burn, who had authored some self-help books, like *I'm O.K., You're O.K.* and *Games People Play*. Each day, members of the community would teach and lecture on one of the subjects that Burn had outlined in his writings.

As I sat in the old school type desk I was listening and taking notes. The lecturer was saying, "As children grow, between the ages of 0 and 6 years old, they start a decisional process with their parents and the outside world called Scripting."

He went on further to teach that, "A script is an ongoing life plan formulated in early childhood, under parental influences, that directs a child's life in the most important aspects of his or her life." He said that sons learn how to be men from their fathers or substitute fathers, and the same happens with mothers and daughters. This seemed to make sense to me. It was somewhat hard to accept, though, when he said we would most likely turn out like our fathers. I knew that I had turned out like my father. I didn't like it, and

I didn't need someone telling me I had. I didn't care much for him. Actually, I hated him.

I was soaking this up. It was clear to me what was being said, and I understood. I particularly liked the study of Game Analysis. A game was an ongoing series of complimentary, ulterior transactions that led to a well defined predictable out come. Oh yes, I knew this. I simply had never heard it put into words so clearly. I thought to myself that this was how I could always predict things people were going to do. It was because I had watched and remembered what they had done. This is why I was convinced that dad had been responsible for my mother's death. He denied it once when I asked him about it. Funny thing was that the same denial, the same demeanor, the same look in his face showed when I had asked him if he had done something else one time. I knew without a doubt he did. Yes, he may not have pulled the trigger, but he had his part in it. I had always thought it odd.

Three men come into your house at five a.m. on the day you're going hunting. Then one of them picks up your pistol and kills your wife while you're still lying in bed. You didn't see anything. Five days later you go to the police station, waving a bible in your hand, and telling the cops, "It was accidental. Please don't charge the guy." I thought that had to have been something. My dad had not at that point in his life ever opened a bible.

Spring was here and I was soon to be released from prison. I was looking forward to getting out and getting started doing something positive. I had to report to a halfway house and wasn't overly excited about that. I had enough of living with character disorders, lunatics and anti-social nut cases. I recalled on many occasions thinking to myself, *some of these people should never get out. Thank God there are prisons.* But that was the condition of my parole, so I could handle it for a few more weeks.

The last day in prison, I was called to the front office. There was a sheriff's deputy standing there. He had come to serve me with a restraining order. According to the order I was ordered by the court not to have any contact with my ex-wife. *Well, that is the way it's going to be,* I thought. She had had an order to bring my little girl to see me once a month, and never did. The only way I ever wanted to see her again anyway was… Oh well, I have changed my way of life. I don't think like that anymore. That's what I kept telling myself anyway. If I had learned anything in treatment it was how to address the voices in my head. It worked for some things, but not everything. I had some discussions about matters and some people too.

The halfway house was everything I thought it would be, so I went with the flow, able to see the light at the end of the tunnel. One night I was sitting there going through the telephone book looking up old friends, namely looking for a girl friend. And then, there it was. One of my old girlfriend's sister's name, Sandy, and her telephone number too. I had always thought she was good looking and so, what was there to lose by calling? Nothing. The phone rang and when she answered I said, "Hello Sandy, how have you been? This is Chuck."

"Chuck who?" she asked, and so I told her. She said, "I don't know you."

So I said, "Oh you must have a boyfriend or something. Sorry, I must have the wrong number," and hung up.

Chapter 32

Life with Sandy

A few nights later I was sitting looking through the phone book again and decided to call Sandy back. Maybe her boyfriend, or whoever he was, wasn't there. She answered the phone and I said, "Sorry I bothered you the other night. This is Chuck. How have you been?"

She responded with, "Who are you and who do you think I am?"

After some small talk I realized that I had in fact dialed the wrong number. She was not who I thought she might be. It didn't seem to really matter to either of us anyway, and so we started to talk. We visited for hours that night. We talked about our lives, places we had been to and all that kind of stuff. Later on, when I hung up the phone, I was feeling pretty good that I had at least a prospect for a woman in my life. So I went to sleep that night, somewhat looking forward to talking with her again the next night.

Sandy and I had been talking over the telephone now for three weeks. Every night we called each other. We were both looking forward to the phone calls and I enjoyed having her company even if it was over the phone. On this night I suggested that we should maybe get together and meet somewhere. I went on to say that my being a stranger and all, perhaps she should bring her brother with her when we met. She said, "You wouldn't care if I did?"

"No," I said, and went on further to say, "And have him bring some of his friends if it would make you feel any better."

With all this said, we agreed to meet me the next night at McDonalds. I thought to myself this was going to be alright. I was wondering what she looked like and was hoping that she was at least good looking. I couldn't sleep that night.

I had met all the requirements at the halfway house and so I was discharged. I had already been spending more and more time at Sandy's house, and she asked me to move in with her, so this was going rather well. It was summertime and I was working construction with a man I met while I was living at the halfway house. This meant getting up very early every morning and driving thirty miles to work, spending the day in the hot humidity and then driving back to the house through rush hour traffic. I had been doing this now for six months and liked the building trade. The pay was the most money I had ever made working a real job. The boss was a good guy and we got along rather well. He worked construction all day and played in a rock and roll band at night. There were some nights that I'm sure he didn't even get any sleep at all. It was his carpentry skills that I liked and he was showing me how to build. I loved the hard work and the thought of my freedom. Prison seemed so far away and I though less about it every day.

One day at work, during my lunch break, I called the house and Sandy was really excited and wanted me to hurry home after work. She stated that she had a great idea that we should drive to North Dakota for the weekend. I said, "Fine with me," and went back to work.

It was hot, humid, and it wasn't long until a thunderstorm came through and there was flash flooding. It had rained for about two hours. It was the hardest rain I had ever seen. I was driving home when the traffic came to a sudden stop. The freeway was under water. I sat there for two more hours waiting for the water to go down and there was no way to make a phone call home. I hoped that Sandy had seen the weather and road report on TV.

Finally, the traffic was moving again and I made it to the house and walked in the door after seven that night. What took place next caught me totally by surprise, and dumbfounded me. Seemed that Sandy had wanted to go to North Dakota and get married. In fact her friends were headed there now and were waiting for us. This was all news to me.

"What took you so long to get here?" she screamed. "Why didn't you call me? I wanted to surprise you. I wanted to go and get married this weekend. Now it's too late". And then she flopped down on the kitchen floor and started pounding her fist and kicking the floor. She was having a tantrum. Crying, yelling and screaming at me. She looked like a two year old sitting there, kicking her feet and pounding her fists on the floor. I couldn't do anything except start laughing. It was the silliest display I had ever seen.

Then she jumped up and started pounding me in the chest yelling, "I hate you, I hate you" and crying more.

"I wanted to get married," she said. She wouldn't stop crying and yelling. She kept having a fit, I was awe struck, and caught by complete surprise. Then the telephone rang. This was a welcome interruption. The drama had been going on now for over an hour. When I answered it, her mother was on the other end and she asked me if child was there.

I said, "Who?"

"Oh, that's what we call Sandy at home. So tell me, are you getting ready to go to North Dakota?" she asked.

Sitting on the deck of the cruise ship, I was relaxing and the waiters were always on time with another Rum Punch. I liked the rum and for a while enjoyed the punch too, until the headache came. Sandy was sun bathing and working on her tan. Seemed that she was always working on her tan and buying another swimsuit.

It had been four months now since we had gotten married, so the cruise was the honeymoon of sorts, I guess. I was hoping that things would work out for us. Sandy was really a nice girl, but we had a shaky start. The wedding was planned to be in front of a judge and my brother was suppose to be the best man. Problem was, he didn't show up. So Sandy's sister stood in his place. This should have been clue number two, but I didn't think much about it. Anyway what was done was done, and here I was sitting in the warm Caribbean sun, smoking some bud and sucking down the Rum Punch. Life couldn't be all that bad. Besides, the tantrum incident was long past and almost forgotten. Then suddenly something dawned on me. I had for a second time married a recovering alcoholic. Another needy woman who had serious unresolved issues with her father. Another nut case. *Funny,* I thought, *they didn't start out this way.* I pondered these thoughts for sometime that day, and seemed to understand the need to have someone fill the void left open from unresolved childhood relationships. I had some myself I guess. I recalled what I had learned in treatment. This was called an unhealthy symbiosis. I got it, but too late. I was living in another codependent relationship, and I didn't like it. Was it love that got me into this, or was it me fulfilling some need of my own to take care of people, to rescue them? *Yes,* I thought, *I was still trying to fill some void in myself.*

Some months later we were remodeling the house and had added on another bedroom. I was putting up some drywall in the back of the house when Sandy came back and out of the blue changed the radio station I was listening to. I didn't give it much thought, but then she came back and unplugged my extension cord too. I wasn't quite sure what this was about. She was still mad that I had a new job with the bondsman and didn't like my being away from home so much. We had been fighting about this for weeks. So, I turned the radio station back to where I had it, plugged the cord back into the outlet and continued to work. Next, she came again and, holding the power cord in her hand, looking at me with an odd expression, unplugged the cord again. Then looking at me she stood there mocking me. "What are you going to do? Come on you sissy. What? Are you afraid of me?"

This was a replay of the way Grandfather was treated by Grandmother, way back in the day. And this kind of thing had been going on for weeks already. I told her to knock it off, or I would give her something to think about, and went back to hanging drywall. I thought she must have gotten my message because she went in to the other room and slammed the door and didn't come back. This had been going on for far too long I thought.

I wanted out of this. I didn't agree with the divorce thing, but I had been here before. Living with a far too needy woman, moody and staring off in to space, acting like a two year old. Come on. I didn't want to be her daddy. I was at the end of my rope.

I was about to continue doing some mudding and taping, when all of a sudden there were two cops that came up from behind me, grabbing hold of my arms and trying to put handcuffs on me. I didn't even know they were there, or why. The next thing I knew there were two more there and they jumped me and knocked me to the floor.

"You're under arrested for domestic abuse," they said.

"What are you talking about?" I asked.

"You made a threat against someone in your house. You're going to jail."

"I'll be out before the ink is dry tough guys," I said as they threw me into the back seat and drove me away in the squad car.

Two days later I was sitting across the desk from my lawyer. I was telling him, "I want out now. I have had enough of this nut case."

He told me that I had a significant amount of money invested in the house and that we should try to recover some of it.

I told him, "I don't want anything except out of this marriage, and make it as fast as possible."

To think that the heat could come into my house and knock me down like I was some punk. I had seen their kind before. I had already been ordered out of the house by the judge. I couldn't go and pick up my belongings without the cops being there, so I washed my hands of that situation. I turned away, never looking back.

Chapter 33

The Ten Thousand Bond

The office was unusually quiet as I walked in on Monday morning. Everyone was busy and the door to Big John's office was closed. That was in itself a sure sign that something was in the air. As I passed the receptionist desk she gave me a smile as she rolled her eyes back toward the boss's office. I had barely sat down to my desk when the office door flew open and the boss called me in to take a seat.

"I won't lose my ten thousand," he told me. "I will not let that little punk rip me off."

And me, not having a clue as to what he was talking about, agreed by shaking my head and saying, "What I can do Big John?"

"I won't have some punk from L.A. come in here and think he can pull some game on me. I want his skin and we won't stop until I get it," he said.

I thought to myself that this was going to be a long week. I said, "Give me the file."

I was told that if I got this *&^%$, there would be a nice bonus for me at the end of the week.

Well, it turned out that John had written another bond that wasn't any good. He was the one that it seemed always did this and it was up to the rest of us to clean up the mess. Last week end the boss worked as was his practice, any time he was getting ready for vacation. The family likes to spend his money and he didn't spare any expense while on a trip. So my job was to fix the problem and put the "mark" in jail. As I looked over the file, the first thing I saw was that the co-signer hadn't signed the deed over for his house. This was the reason for the anger. This was an unsecured bond. In the bail bond business this was a no-no. And to further complicate matters we were not even sure if the "mark" had given us his real name. I started by getting all I could on the co-signer and found that he was employed with the Ford automotive plant. This was good to know until I checked and found that he was off work on disability. Damn, I thought. I would have to run a game on this chump.

I called the co-signer and told him that I was with the Ford insurance office and said that we were checking up to see if he was getting his checks on time for being off work. "Hell no," he told me. He said that he had been waiting for weeks to get paid and that all he was getting was the run around.

Right on, I thought. I assured him that I would be in town tomorrow and in fact would stop over to see him, and if it was alright I could help straighten things out for him. "Oh by the way," I told him, "It looks like some of your paper work was not signed. I'll see you in the morning say about ten?"

He agreed.

I was on a roll now, and I had to keep the motion going. As I was leaving the office to work my game I turned and reassured my boss, "I'll take care of it for you, Big John."

I didn't have much time to make my plan work, and if it was going to work at all, I would need some official looking papers. I headed for the state employment office. After looking through the forms they had in the bins, I took what I thought I could use and headed back to the office. I started typing in the spaces with the co-signers name and other information we had in the file. Then I put an X next to where he would have to sign to get his benefits. Next I got a release of property form from our file and a quick claim form and put an X on them as well. Now if all went the way I had it planned, I would have Big John's ten grand secure.

As I pulled up to the office the next day, I was looking forward to getting this paper signing thing finished because I had to go find the "mark" and throw his tail in jail. I went in to the office and got Big John's car keys and headed out for my appointment. John always had a nice, new car and today wasn't any different. Here I was driving the bosses brand new Cadillac. No one drove John's car and here I was. I needed to look the part as I cinched up my tie looking in the mirror. *You look good,* I thought. *Now, let's go and run the game.* I was a perfect fit for the skip trace business, and I loved what I was doing. I mean I had only been out of prison two years, and now I was playing the same old games and getting paid to do it. How sweet is that and I loved my get out of jail free card.

As I pulled up to the front of the man's house he met me at the door and welcomed me in. He offered me some coffee as I sat down to get his signature. I explained how sorry I was that the office had made a mistake and that I was there to make sure that we got everything we needed in order, and that he would get what he had coming. I really had to put myself in check to stop from laughing. I loved this. I started by reading some of the papers I had gotten from the employment office with the state logo on the letterhead. I read to him about an employee's right to Workers Compensation and asked if he understood what I was saying. I made it clear to mention that he had rights and he nodded. Then I said, "Well, if we can finish up here before noon, I'll fax these papers to the main office and you should get your money as early as tomorrow's mail."

With that said, he signed the papers, told me thank you, and out the door I went thinking to myself, *stupid!* Hey I didn't feel bad for the guy. He would never know what had happened and hopefully his employer would have his money in the mail anyway. I was working for the bail bondsman. After all, that was who paid me. I loved my job. Sure beat sitting in the joint.

As I walked into the office the mood changed as I handed the signed papers to John. It seemed that I had changed the atmosphere in the whole place. The boss was walking back and forth with a big smile, waving the signed papers, telling everyone how valuable I was to his organization, and that he could count on me. I liked working for John and was sure of one thing. He would never let me sit in jail. As soon as the excitement had died down it was back to locating the "mark" and bringing him before the judge before the time ran out.

I had been on this bond case for almost two weeks with not as much as a lead. It seemed that this punk had disappeared and no one was saying a word. By now surely someone was talking, but not in this case. So we had to put the word out on the street that afternoon that there was a five hundred dollar reward for information as to where we could find Jonny Fred Whitman. All cash and no questions asked. As the day was getting later John got a call from another bondsman in Los Angeles telling him that our guy had been spotted there and so John caught the late flight to the west coast.

I have had some strange days working bonds and this day was about to take the cake. The big boss was on the telephone from L.A., sitting on a stake out, when a woman entered the office and told me that she knew where to find Jonny Whitman. I told John that I needed to go and that I would call him back in a short while. This woman was seated at my desk holding a small child as she asked me if what she had heard was true. Was there a five hundred dollar reward for this guy? I told her that I hoped that she was not playing me because I didn't have time for Bullwinkle. She asked me again about the money and I told her that what she had heard was true, there was a reward. She went on to explain that she stayed in the same house as him, and that in fact he would be back tonight. This was most interesting, John in L.A. following up on a lead and now this. As I asked more questions I was concerned about her safety, but she informed me that she would be O.K. and that no one would ever know that she had been here. I told her that if what she told me was so, that I would give her the money in the morning. As she left the office I was back on the telephone with Big John giving him the new information. He said put a plan together, so I went to work. I didn't have my forty five automatic with me today, didn't think I would need it, but I had earlier in the week purchased a .357 that was still in my desk, so I would have to carry it tonight.

I was sitting three or four parking places from the front of the building in my car with Dan, Big Johns brother. We had three more guys in another car sitting around the corner. The plan we made with the informant was that she would leave the down stairs door open for us and when we saw the "mark' and his friend enter the building. We were to give her enough time to take the baby to the back room. I was going to be point man, so I would enter first. As we walked up the stairs we could hear people talking as the music was playing. I had my firearm in my hand as I kicked the door down and yelled," Bondsman everyone down on the floor, on the floor now!" There was the "mark" running to the kitchen I went after him and tripped on a rug when, my gun went off and he fell to the floor. Dan ran into the room as the guy lay on the floor. We looked at each other thinking that I had shot and killed him. I holstered my gun and went down on one knee to hand cuff the guy. As it turned out he wasn't shot. I rolled him over and I picked him up to walk out the door. On the way down the steps to the waiting car, one of the other guys made a play at me. So I threw the guy in handcuffs to the floor for Dan to watch as I ran this punk's head into the wall, but that wasn't all he had coming as he pulled a long syringe out of his pants and tried to stick me. I grabbed his arm, threw him in to the wall and showed him some old school with a good tail kicking. Down to the car we went and I started the drive to the office. I loved it! I was so jacked up. I felt like superman, the adrenalin was flowing hard. My heart was pounding fast. Yes, I got you punk, looking at him through the rear view mirror. Yes, you are my paycheck this week.

We were back downtown when Dan called the boss and told him that we had caught the "mark." We were standing in Big John's office and put the telephone on speaker so we could all hear the call. Then John said, "You thought you could out run me you little son@#@#$%? Well what do you have to say for yourself? Well, come on! Nothing to say?"

The guy wouldn't answer, when all of a sudden Big John said, "Chuck, double him over."

So he got it in the guts not once, but twice; one for the boss man and one for me.

Chapter 34

Jimmy the Car Salesman

I still recall the first time I met Jim. He was the salesman at the car lot where I purchased my pick-up truck. I remember that day well. As we made the deal, I told him, "You get the price down by three thousand dollars and when we close the deal I'll give you five hundred cash."

He loved this and I drove off with the truck. I remember that day and the look on his face when I asked him, "What is it that you think I do for a living?"

It was funny the way he answered me with "I'm not sure, but I could about imagine."

My response was, "I am a skip tracer."

"You mean you're a bounty hunter?" he asked.

My answer to that question was always the same, as I had been asked it before many times. So I said, "Some people call it that, but in the business, we prefer to be called skip tracers."

And so began the relationship with Jimmy, the used car salesman and me. Jim liked my style and I'm sure he was feeling as if he was now part of some movie or something. The drama and wanting to hear about my latest arrest would often be what we talked about. And so before long we were having coffee on a regular basis.

Today, however, he had something on his mind when called and asked if I could meet and have breakfast with him. I said, "Sure, are you buying?"

As I walked into the café, Jim was sitting with some of the regulars that gathered there every morning. I always got a kick out of the way they viewed me. Or perhaps it was Jim's stories about me, because when they saw me walk in they always got up and went to another table.

As I sat down Jim poured me a cup of coffee from the pot on the table and then asked if I would rather have the waitress bring some fresh. I assured him that this was fine and as the waitress stood there I ordered my breakfast. So after some small talk I asked, "So what's up?"

Jim was looking around to make sure no one was looking or listening in on our conversation as he began his reason for calling me today. "Well," he began, "I'm having a problem with my daughter and I need some help in dealing with it. Actually, it's not really her," he said, "but her boy friend."

He continued to tell me how the boyfriend was slapping his daughter around and that he had said something to him about it, only to hear something like get out of my face and mind your own business. As our waitress set my meal down, Jim took another look around the room as to make sure we were still not being overheard.

"Well, Jimmy, what do you think I can do to help you?" I asked, as he assured me that he knew that I would know how to handle the problem for him.

"So what would you like me to do, and how soon would you like to have it done?"

"I want you to teach him a lesson and I would like you to do it before my birthday." It seemed that his daughter would be over to his house for the party. Somehow she would know then that he had "friends with muscle" was my guess.

"Jim," I said, "I'll see that it is taken care of and I'll need to see that five hundred back."

We shook hands as I reminded him of the rules, "Don't call me, and don't ever talk about it."

Jim assured me he understood as we shook hands and parted ways.

As with every job, I had done my homework and this had required some stake out time to see when the "mark" was coming and going, what the neighborhood was like, and to plan the escape. With all that in place I parked one block over from the house on a one-way street and I would leave that way as I knew the heat would have to come from only one direction, and that was from behind my location. I had left the car in a store parking lot this was a short walk from the house and I would leave the keys and anything from my pockets in the glove compartment. When the job was finished I could walk and not be seen leaving the house, get it the car and leave. As I walked up to the front door of the house I stood and listened for a few minutes to get a feel for the place. Everything looked good as I knocked on the door waiting for it to open I was thinking to myself that I hope the mark answers the door as this would mean one less witness that could identify me if something went wrong. I no longer had the thought when the door opened, and he was standing there right it front of me. "I think I backed into your car," I said.

As he closed the door behind him looking toward where his car was parked and then I started firing him up and knocked him to the ground and I pounded him some more. The fight was already out of him as I pounded him some more saying, "How does it feel to be beat on? Do you like hitting women, you sissy? You little punk! If you ever hit her again I'll be back. Don't you dare touch her, you punk! You woman beater." As I was punching him some more I knew that he wouldn't be a boyfriend to this girl much longer. "Do you hear me? Do you want me to come visit you again? I'll be watching you. I know your every move, got it?"

I got up from on top of him and headed for my car, climbed in and drove off. I could already hear the sirens from the cop cars coming. As I took off my gloves and pulled into to the flow of traffic driving away to have something to eat, I was thinking to myself that it was an easy five hundred and congratulating myself for doing a good night's work.

One week later I pulled into the car lot and was looking at some new pickups as Jimmy came out and asked me if I needed some help. I stated that I was looking for a car for my daughter and, yes, I could use some help. With all the chitchat out of the way he told me that his birthday was great and that he had gotten everything that he had wished for. I said, "Well good for you, and happy birthday."

It seemed that Jimmy was especially proud of the black eyes the boyfriend was wearing, and I could see that he felt like he had done something for his little girl. I was glad that I was able to help a friend and knew that if I needed Jim for anything I would have it. I just never knew when I would need an alibi for something or could use a car for the day. Jim was a friend and a good resource. If I ever needed to call on him he would be there. He was now in my pocket and I liked it.

Chapter 35

Coke, Crank and Dealing with Punks

I should have never trusted the guy anyway, I thought to myself. I had met him in the joint a few years earlier and then I had bumped into him on the street. We exchanged some conversation and it was clear to me then that he was in some bad shape from drug use, so I invited him to stay at my house until he could clean up his act and kick the dope. It was the least I could do to help someone in need and this guy was in some bad shape. I had plans to be out of town for the weekend anyway, so this would work out for him as well as me. He had reassured me that he really wanted some help that he could care for my house while I was gone, and then thanked me for my help.

On Monday when I returned from being out of town the first thing that I noticed was that my car was gone. Then when I entered my house it was apparent that I had been ripped off of all my valuables. I was, to say the least, not happy. Everything I had acquired since the divorce from Sandy was gone. I was extremely angry and all I wanted was to find this punk. I knew when I left him at the house that something would go bad, I could feel it.

I knew that the first thing I needed to do was to locate my car. The rest would follow after that, and I had business with this punk. How dare he, after my kindness, steal my property and use me like some kind of a trick. All I could think of was beating his head in. When I found my car it was where I thought it would be, so I got in it and drove it to a friend's house. Then I checked it out to make sure it was in good shape and that there was no dope stashed in it. That's all I would need would be a dope beef I thought, of course it was out of gas.

This guy and his friends used Meth and cooked coke down to make crack and smoked it in a pipe. So checking out the car was a smart move, least something be hid in it. Next, I knew that I would need some back up, so I called a friend for some help. My partner and I had my two-way radios and the police scanner to keep in touch and listen for the heat. So while he was covering the back of the house and doing look out, I would burst through the front door. I stood there outside listening for a few moments. I could hear two people talking inside, so I busted down the door and went in to clean house. The mark saw me, and a sound from deep in his gut came out of his mouth as he tried to get up from the couch. I threw a television at him hitting him in the face and knocking him to the floor, kicking him as hard and fast as I could. His buddy made a move at me as I smashed him in the face with the VCR, he was out on the floor, but for good measure I kicked him in the face to make sure he would be no problem. The mark was now in the kitchen trying to rip a leg off of the table that was turned upside down, his eyes were wide open with a mix of rage, dope and fear as I kicked him in the head and proceeded to give him some old school; we were on the floor up against the back door and so my partner couldn't get in. Then I grabbed an extension cord and wrapped it around his neck holding him tightly with one hand, twisting the cord tighter as he turned blue. I asking politely for my stuff back, whispered in his ear, telling him that his time was up, pulling his face closer, so he could see the look in my eyes. It's in a box in the closet he pleaded, the other stuff he said had been sold. I let him slowly pass out before letting the cord go, he fell to the floor. School was over for the day. Class dismissed.

I could hear the sound of the other people in the building coming to see what was going on. We also knew that someone would have by now called the heat, so we got into my car and left. I had turned left down a street as a cop car passed me with his lights on driving fast to where we had just left. I had the police scanner on and heard the dispatcher give them a description of my car as soon as I passed them, so I turned left again and drove to another friend's house and parked in his garage and closed the door.

Three days later I was sitting in my house having some coffee when my partner came running in the door. "The cops are down stairs," he said, "and they are headed up here."

There was a knock at the door as my friend jumped out the window to the ground. I opened the door and was face to face with two cops. They were there to arrest me for assault. Sitting in the cell, I didn't have much to worry about and I knew it. My story was good, and it was true. I went to recover my property that was taken. I explained to the detective the whole story from start to finish. Then I told him to go to the Target store and pick up the film I had taken there for development, and he would see what had been taken from my house. As it was I had taken pictures of all my property for my renter's insurance policy and hadn't picked them up yet. I had proof of everything I was saying.

Three days later the detective came to the cell and told me that all the charges had been dropped and stated that he didn't really believe everything I had told him. He said that I couldn't be the only person that kicked down the door, inflicted so much damage on those two guys, and destroyed the house in such a short amount of time. Further, he said that the victims had given him false names and that he couldn't find them. It seemed that they were part of an elaborate check-writing scheme and were wanted by the police themselves.

I decided that it was time for a change. I had enough of the fast lane for a while and all the craziness that went along with it. So I packed up all my belongings and made a move to see my dad for a while. I had saved some money and thought I would go down and buy myself a small piece of land and kick back. I needed some time to plan for something different in my life. The way things were going I'd end up back in prison for a long time. I had developed a attitude that I didn't care anymore.

Chapter 36

Meeting Diana

Standing on the top of a hill early in the morning I was looking out over the Mississippi River Valley. *Yes,* I thought, *this spot would suit me well.* I would have a southeastern exposure, and that would work well for a garden spot. I could build a large garage and have my living quarters in the back, and settle here until I could build myself a house. I could do some woodworking on the side and make a good income working construction. This would be home. It had been over a year since the divorce from Sandy, and I was able to save almost eight grand. I was doing all right I thought. I was staying at my dad's for the time being and had a nice little job coming up this weekend.

I had given Big John my notice at work and I hadn't used any coke for almost a year now. I had learned some lessons in the last year and one big one was that coke was deceptive. Yes it all sounded good. Buy a quarter ounce for five hundred and make eight selling it. I thought I'd make some fast money. Problem was I started using the stuff and I liked it too much and I was using up all my profit. I was always making some fast money, but spent it as fast as I made it. A line of coke and a couple shots of vodka, and I felt powerful. Nothing could stand in my way. And the bail bonding, well it was a great job. I loved it. The pay, the action and all the late night stakeouts… I think I was born for skip tracing work. I loved the fast lane and the feeling of all the action, however I was going too fast and had a near wreck. And the shooting on my last bounty job… What if I had killed the guy? And being a felon in possession of a handgun? I'd been there before. It was good to have it all in the past and I was convinced if I kept it up I'd wind up dead. *Yes,* I thought to myself *this is where I never turn back. Leave it all in the past, a new start.*

As I arrived at the work site early, I realized that I had a lot to accomplish today. I was the only paid guy on the job and so I was hired to lead the work crew today. Now, I was ready to get the show on the road. All the others guys were friends of the owners, or owed them some favors. Either way I was ready to get started. I had the layout marked and was pulling up the roof trusses, putting them in to position, while the other guys nailed them into place. This kind of work is not so hard, but one needs to be careful and pay attention, or you could get hurt. The project was going well and by now it was about time for lunch break. Some of the help had been drinking beer already, or maybe they hadn't stopped from the night before. Hard to tell. But in my opinion, power saws, working on a roof and booze didn't mix. I had said something already to one guy, but I didn't come down too hard. If it wasn't that I needed the help, I would have sent these jokers down the road.

It was lunchtime when the owner of the house introduced me to a friend she had already told me about. She said, "You will really like her. She is pretty and a real nice person and I have told her about you too."

I had seen her pull up in her little black convertible earlier while I was on the roof, and she looked alright to me. She had a bright smile and it was obvious to me that she had some style from the way she conducted herself. She had a way she kind of turned her head. It caught my eye. So as we were introduced she put her hand out for me to shake, and for whatever reason I didn't take it. I think I was a little intimidated by her or something. I said nice to meet you, smiled and went back to work. I thought about it later. I was really off my game. And I didn't make much of an impression on her at all. *Oh well,* I thought *I had work to do*. But I was sure that I would be talking with her later. I thought that she had pretty blue eyes.

Back up on the roof we worked all day, setting roof trusses and then sheeting them. Now it was starting to get dark, I wanted to get this job finished, I was close, and all I had left to do was to lay down some felt paper.

I had been keeping my eye on Diana all day because she had really gotten my attention. When I saw her get into her car and drive off, I wasn't sure I would see her later. I even asked someone if she was coming back and I was told that she was. *Good* I thought. Then a little later, as I was eating some supper and having a beer, the lady in the black convertible drove up again, only this time I was going to make some conversation. I liked the way she looked and she had some self-confidence. I liked that.

I wasn't the only guy there that wanted to talk to Diana. There was this joker that had been trying to get her attention all afternoon and by now, dude was half smashed and acting like an idiot. He even had some unbecoming language coming out of his mouth. Then he started to tell some poorly worded jokes, so I moved a little closer to him and looking around said, "Pal, you need to go home, now! I don't want to turn around and see you again"

Seems he got the message loud and clear, and left. And with that, stupid was out of the way and the others were following suit and taking their good old boy humor and moving on to something else. It wouldn't be too long now, and I would be visiting with Diana and may be playing my guitar, singing some old songs. The night was still early, oh yes. We sat and visited for hours, singing some songs and then we went for a walk. The evening was really nice as we walked and talked about nice things, making comments about houses we saw along the way. We both went separate ways that evening, having made plans to have lunch the next day.

Diana and I had been seeing each other for a couple of months and I was really enjoying my time spent with her. She was a really sweet woman that had lived in the area most of her life and all her family lived here, as did her grandmother. Every morning she would go to her grandmother's house to visit and help her with things around the house and do the cooking. It was clear to me that she loved her grandmother a lot the way she talked about her and cared for her. This morning I was with Diana visiting too. It was funny the way grandmother looked at me. She reminded me of the way my grandmother looked at me, with eyes that could see right through me. I was sure to mention to her that my intentions were good and she gave me a sweet little chuckle as if to say, "Sure they are." I had a nice afternoon sitting there listen to her grandmother tell me stories about Diana growing up and answering her question about me. I really tried to be as honest as I could and I think at the end of the day I had won her over.

Chapter 37

On the Run from Minnesota

I had just pulled in a Northern Pike and this was the sixth one for me today. Fishing was great I thought, as I guided the boat over the lake headed for another marshy inlet that would take us to yet another lake. We were fishing in Northern Minnesota in the Crow Wing Chain of the upper Mississippi river. Now it was early July. That meant it was hot, muggy and humid. Even out here on the lake we were cooking. There was another heat on my mind this afternoon however, and that was the court hearing that was coming up in a few days.

The cops had pulled me over a few months ago for speeding and when he ran my name I was flagged and to find out had an arrest warrant. I went to jail that night and sat there for an hour until my buddy bailed me out. I had made some good friends in the bail bond business and they wouldn't let me sit. Well to find out the punk that ripped me off a year ago had written some check with my name and cashed them with my driver's license. He had removed my picture and pasted one of his on the card. He and his accomplishes had used it and cashed tens of thousands of dollars in stolen checks. He had set me up to take the fall. I wasn't going to jail, that's all there was to it.

It was raining and storming outside so tonight would be spent in the cabin playing board games and singing along with the radio. I was as relaxed as I could ever remember being here tonight with the four of us, Diana, her daughter Stacy and son William. I had always wanted a family like this and I wasn't going to do anything to lose this relationship. I had fallen in love with Diana and with the two kids. The only one that was missing in my life now was my daughter Jacqueline. And after the last visit we had with her I doubted that I would see her for a while. So tonight we would have to talk about court. Seems that we had been avoiding the subject. I had already made up my mind of course that I wasn't going to jail. The hearing was in a few days.

I didn't like any judge as I had seen my share of them, and I had an even lower opinion of county attorneys. And now in a few days I would have to stand in front of both of them. The judge on his bench in his black robe, acting like he was some kind of a God… And the D.A. looked like one of those guys that had to give up his lunch money at school. He was a district attorney so he could get back at the kind of guys that used to beat him up. There was even something about the sound of it - *the bench.* I had less than a little respect for the man. I had none. I had watched these clowns wheel and deal for years with the lives of people, with no sense of compassion at all. Sitting above you, judging you with their law. There wasn't one that much cared about anything other than themselves, and not one that ever did anything for me.

We had already developed a great relationship, Diana and I, so everything was open for discussion, as was the felony I was charged with in Minneapolis circuit court. I hadn't done anything I was charged with. If I was guilty, it was for trusting someone that didn't have their proving time in. Little did I know that when my house was ripped off it would still be causing me problems now but it was and I was having those conversations again in my mind. This time the thoughts were taking me to the next level, to a place that really had me questioning and wondering about myself and the kind of things I was capable of doing. The only way to deal with people like this was to dig a hole. You couldn't reason with them. They were in a class with Barbara. They use and abuse you. The thoughts came easy and the solution for the problem seemed simple enough. Yet each time I would think about it I found myself feeling sorry for them, writing them off in my mind. *Turn my back and don't look back.*

I had long since made up my mind that I wasn't going to jail and we were making plans of where we would go, if things went bad and the D.A. wanted to send me to jail. So with the U.S. map laid on the table I handed the boot piece from the monopoly game to Stacy. She stood in one spot as I turned her around a few times blindfolded, then she tossed the boot on to the map.

We had all agreed that where the boot landed, that is where we would move to. As she opened her eyes we all looked on as the boot was on top of a place called Hoquiam, Washington. I recall us talking about how to pronounce the name, turned out Diana and Stacy had it right.

The next morning we drove to town where Stacy had an appointment to take her road test for her driver's license. While she was doing this Diana and I were going to start making contacts in Washington. We started with a call to the chamber of commerce for some information, and called a realtor looking for a house to live in once we made the trip. We didn't have much time until my July 7 court date as it was already the third of the month.

I had already found us a house. Furthermore, we could live there rent-free. It seemed the owners wanted someone to do some remodeling for them. This sounded good for us, as I had the carpentry experience and so we were good to go. We were all full of excitement as the conversation was about the adventure we were going to take.

That night we drove to the city and checked into a hotel. After dinner we drove to the train station and got me a one-way ticket to Shelby, Montana. This is where we would meet up if I had to make a break for it. The ticket was in my new name, Timothy C. Dunn. I had found this name in the newspaper obituaries section. Then I went to the state office of vital statistics and paid to have a copy of the birth certificate. Next I went and applied for a new state I.D. card. And so with that I was a new man. I was leaving the old life behind me and starting fresh - new family and all. There was a sense of freedom that had come over me and I loved it. I was really looking forward to moving to Washington. I had spent the summer there once with Grandmother and Grandfather and was excited about going back. That night I found it hard to sleep, partly from the drama and partly from the fear of something happening to our plans that would keep me from making the trip west. Then there was the possibility of something going wrong and my being sent to prison.

Early the next morning, as we finished breakfast, we went over the plan once again. Now it was time to drive down town to the courthouse. I had been here on many court dates before as a bond agent, but this was a first time here for I was here for myself. As we found the courtroom there was my attorney. Charley had defended me more than once over the years in other matters and our relationship was good. The rule was never to lie to your lawyer unless you had no other choice, so Charley knew everything. I always found that if my lawyer believed in me, he would fight harder.

Two years earlier Charley defended me in a case that could have sent me up then too. I remember the day all to well. I thought I was going to do time, so on the morning before court I didn't have the money to pay my attorney fees. I did have a new computer that had never been taken out of the box. I asked him if this would make us even. He accepted and I got six months in jail. It sure could have been worse. Judges don't like to be lied to and I was charged with perjury.

So here I was again and it didn't look good. Right before lunch Charley came and sat down to talk. He told us that the District Attorney wouldn't deal and was going to ask for five years straight with any plea deal. "Five years," I said.

I didn't even have a thing to do with what I was charged with. The charge was aggravated forgery. Didn't matter. I was convicted once before for forgery in the deal with Susan and dad, so that was enough for the State Attorney to believe I was guilty. Take five years or face much more time.

"Charley," I said, "go tell him that I'll give them my answer after the lunch hour. Oh and by the way, I won't be there, so it has been nice knowing you. I'm out of here." We shook hands as he wished us the best and we turned and got into the elevator. Once the door closed I changed clothes and put on a hat and some sunglasses. We got off the elevator, left the building and walked to where the car was parked and drove directly to the hotel. I knew that as soon I didn't appear for court that a warrant would be issued for my arrest. That evening I boarded the Amtrak train for Shelby, Montana. This is where Diana and the kids would meet up with me in three days. The train ride took about twenty hours and I think I slept the whole ride. I was beat and drained of all energy.

Chapter 38

Hoquiam, Salvation 10-11-90

Standing in the yard of our new home I could see the harbor from here. The smell of the sea breeze smelled good and filled my senses and I loved it. It had been a good trip from Minnesota and the heat hadn't pulled us over. I was free! I knew that there would be a warrant out for my arrest, but "Chuck" was long gone and after all I was Tim Dunn. I had a Washington license and was getting used to the new name. Really I liked it. I was a new man. I had taken my old life and buried it deep in the back of my mind. I had clean slate and no one was the wiser.

We spent the next weeks cleaning our new house and the yard, working hard to make it our home. The owners of the house stopped by to introduce themselves to us and to have me sign a renter's type agreement. I liked signing my new name, yet I felt odd in doing so. *What is this thing I'm feeling guilty about* I thought. *So what if it's not my real name, I have identification.* I recall that afternoon Diana was calling me Chuck instead of Tim. I had asked her to go along with me on this. Later when I asked why, she stated to me, "You will always be Chuck to me." *Well,* I thought, *that was my middle name now. It would be easy enough to explain. That was my dad's name. Everyone called me Chuck at home.*

It was summer in the Pacific Northwest and so the weather was great. We spent days at the beach picking up sand dollars and seashells. I would share with Diana and the kids how I used to do, earlier this year while visiting my dad's mom and dad here at this same beach. Things seemed to be going so well for me here, yet I continued to have thoughts of being arrested and taken back to jail. I really didn't want anything to ruin the new life we had put together. I was always looking around expecting something to happen. It dawned on me that I had experienced these feelings before, and I wouldn't let them get to me. It was weakness to be scared. I am not weak. *Buck up* I thought.

Diana had gotten a job and the kids were in school now and I was working for a man in an appliance shop repairing washers and dryers. The pay was cash so there were no taxes to pay, and no way to trace it. One afternoon walking home, I met a man in the alley by the house, and it didn't take long to sum him up. So that night I had a bag of pot to smoke, oh yes. I was feeling pretty good now. Some good smoke sure made things easier for me. I could think well, work faster. My conversation was more fun than it had been for weeks. *Yes,* I thought, *I would always smoke pot.* It slowed me down just a little, took off the edge. Pot was good for me. This stuff tasted pretty good to me. Actually it was the best I had ever smoked. I had after all smoked it long enough that I should know. I recalled when I was in the treatment program back in prison. All the guys in the group were yelling and screaming at me. They didn't like it when I made the statement, "I'll always smoke weed."

Funny I thought how fast time had gone by. Here it was October already. I wasn't quite ready for the amount of rain we were getting. It didn't seem to stop, day and night blowing wind. I have never seen so much rain in my life. Oh well. Out to the garage I would go and smoke some weed. This was what I needed. I loved smoking. Grass was the drug for me. The dope really helps me with the thoughts I was having. The battles in my mind continued and they were more and more violent. I wanted to go back to Minnesota and take care of some people that needed some schooling. I found it harder and harder to get these things out of my mind. On some days all I thought was why I didn't kill Barbara that night at the top of the stairs and asking myself lots of questions like that. These thoughts would come out of nowhere. I wasn't really thinking them myself. Somehow they showed up in my mind uninvited and would consume me.

A few days earlier I had seen an ad in the paper for a male Cocker Spaniel puppy. I thought, *I would like a pup,* so I went to get this cute little dog. The first time I tried to pet him he bit me, but I thought *He'll be okay. He has probably been hit and hurt by someone.* So I took him home that day and named him Spike. Fitting name

I thought for a dog that would dare to bite me. I sat holding Spike for days, loving him up, watching TV. I didn't want to leave the front of the television. We were at war and the pictures were all too real. Bombs with camera mounted on them blowing up buildings, tanks speeding through the desert and all unfolding in front of me on television. *Is this the end of the world?* I thought. It is after all going to take place in the Middle East. I thought about some of the things I had heard in church with Grandmother in Florida about this - how all the armies of the world would gather, or something like that. So I sat back feeling good watching T.V. and smoking some bud for hours at a time.

My new dog needed a bath. He was stinking. So with some dog shampoo in one hand and Spike under my arm, up the stairs to the bathtub we went. As the tub was filling with water I was petting the dog and loving him up but he was shaking and looking scared. As soon as I put him in the tub of water he nipped me on the hand, so I slapped him and continued to bathe him when he bit me again. This time I was mean to the little dog and hit him harder than I had to. I had hurt him and he was shaking now and looking at me with hopelessness on his face. I started to have tears in my eyes thinking how I had hurt him. As I dried him off with a towel I kept crying and feeling guilty for what I had done to him. I picked him up, walked down the stairs, got a leash and headed out the door.

Here I was crying and sobbing like a baby over a dog that shouldn't have bit me anyway. I walked for many blocks as the wind and rain blew in my face. The tears were rolling down my cheeks, being lost in the raindrops, when all of a sudden I realized I had walked some distance. I found myself at a local pier along the river. I was standing there alone with the dog looking out over the water as I began crying out loud. I was weeping, sobbing uncontrollably. The emotion and tears continued to pour out of me. I was bawling like a baby. My chest was heaving upward with each breath. I couldn't catch my breath. I was looking out over the water as the words came out of my mouth, "God I need you, oh please God help me." As I was weeping harder and harder, sobbing. All of a sudden every bad thing I had ever done in my life was coming to memory as I cried. All the people I had hurt, the crimes I had committed. Everything I was ever guilty of was right before me as I pleaded with God for help. I was weeping uncontrollably and my guts were in pain. Soon I began to feel an emptiness within me. I had, in a few moments of time, poured out everything in my life, every evil deed, every crime I had ever committed, every person I had hurt came to mind, and then I called out from the depth of my soul, the bottom of my heart and said, "In Jesus name, God help me please. I am so scared. Please forgive me oh God for what I have done. Please, I am so sorry."

I wept there for what seemed hours, pouring everything out, when all of a sudden calmness seemed to slowly move upon me, consuming me, and my mind was clear. The air of the night was still. The rain had stopped. I was breathing in the fresh clean air and then a peace began to flow in to me. I could feel it entering my body, filling me up. I was free. I had never been in this state before. I could feel the presence of God in my midst. My mind was clear, at ease. I felt clean, and I was free. Now the tears that flowed were tears of gratitude and thankfulness. I was smiling and thanking God. I have never felt so complete and at ease with in myself. I was clean inside. I didn't feel high anymore and I found myself praising God. I walked into the night a new man.

Chapter 39

Woman, Goat and Church

The next day I was still filled with the great joy I had found the night before at the pier. My level of excitement was at its highest point in my life. I was thanking God out loud and in my heart all day long, praising Him for the forgiveness I had received last night.

This was all very new for my family and me. Diana was understanding and accepting of all I was sharing, and even encouraging. I think the kids thought my newfound faith somewhat overwhelming. I wanted everyone to have what I had found. I thought that they should trust and believe in God like I did. I was pumped and didn't want to think about anything else except what had happened to me. I must have been overbearing to say the least.

I had found the Christian Broadcasting Network on the television, and was watching it for hours on end. I was soaking in all I could about this new life with God I had discovered. I was thanking Jesus, singing old hymns I had heard with grandmother at her church. There were still tears of gratitude and thankfulness rolling down my face. I was crying and feeling good at the same time. This must be what the preacher on the television was talking about, "the peace that surpasses all understanding." I had found freedom and now there were the thoughts coming to my mind that I need to go to a church. I had spent some time talking with Diana and talked to her about my desire to go to church. She said that if I felt that I needed to do that, then I should. So I planned on going the next morning and couldn't get it off my mind.

Here I sat in church on a Sunday morning feeling good about being here and uncomfortable at the same time. I had not been there long when the preacher came out and started talking. I wanted to hear some more. I had been listening to the guys on TV and what they were saying seemed to agree with me. I didn't think about it much then but, I am sure that I really had Diana and the kids wondering if may be I hadn't gone off the deep end, that perhaps I had gone crazy on them. I had in the last thirty hours brought some big drama and disruption to the household. So I sat through the service, sang some songs and when it was over met some people, shook hands and headed out the door.

I walked toward the car thanking God for loving me and for saving my soul. I was thinking that it had been only three months ago we were headed to Washington, me wanted by the law and Diana and the kids trusting and believing in me, and willing to change the life they had known so well for me. We had a home together and life was going well. I was in love with Diana and realized how special of a person she was. I was truly fortunate to have such a wonderful lady to spend my life with. I wondered if she would meet Jesus too. I hoped she would. She was already the nicest, kindest person I had ever known.

I was walking down the street when all at once, having no longer had these thoughts, there out of no where was a young woman dressed in a pure white bright gown walking toward me on the sidewalk. She seemed to not even be touching the ground. The wind was blowing her long, blond hair up and back off her shoulders as she walked past me, while leading a white Billy goat with long horns with a rope in her hand. I turned back to see where she was going and she was gone as fast as I had first seen her. Then, right then, I heard the voice I had listened to two nights ago say to me, "Don't come back here anymore"

Chapter 40

Going to Church

All day long I had been thanking God and watching the Christian television show *Praise the Lord*. The people were showing so much love for one another and with compassion they reached out to the viewers. The words and message hit home with me. I was continuing to weep throughout the day. The tears were flowing like they had a few nights ago at the pier, yet I was at peace. I was crying with gratitude for all God had done in my life a few nights ago. So I went to the bedroom and closed the door because I didn't want anyone to see or hear me.

I continued to pray and thank God for all He had done for me, and I cried and cried for an hour until my guts hurt. There weren't any thoughts coming to my mind. It was raw emotion and the valve was open all the way. I felt spent, completely void of any guilt or sin. I realized that I needed to talk to someone about what was going on in my life, maybe a pastor or a minister or someone like that. It was almost nine at night, but I knew that I wanted to call someone. I started looking through the phone book and came to the church section, as I ran my fingers down the page, I stopped, and dialed the number I saw there.

To my welcome surprise someone answered the telephone and I didn't know really what to say. Running through my mind were the events of the past few days and everything I had been watching on television, so I asked the man, "Are you a spirit-filled Church?"

His answer was, "Well what do you mean by spirit-filled? If you're asking do we trust in the Spirit of God then yes, we are."

At that moment I was filled with more excitement as I talked with the pastor. He was very kind and asked me my name and I told him, "Tim Dunn." He then invited me to join him and others at the next meeting on Wednesday evening. I had no sooner hung up the phone, than I started to experience something that would further alter the course of my life.

All of a sudden from out of nowhere there were voices in my mind that were not of my own thought. Not like the voices in the conversations I use to have in my mind, but this was much different. I attempted to think about something else, but to no avail. I was, I thought, having a battle within my own mind, with myself, arguing back and forth. Then I could hear other voices too, lots of voices, not with my ears, but within me somehow. They were very real. What I was hearing was something or someone saying, "Call the cops now, and tell them you're wanted by the law in Minnesota.

You're a liar, you're no Christian. Look at all the things you have done, you stabbed the guy in the chest for attacking you, remember when you burned down that garage? Call the Pastor and tell him that, see if he wants you at his church then."

And I was hearing screaming, yelling, and ridicule, voices laughing at me, making fun of me. I felt like I was starting to go crazy. It was like I was awake and having a nightmare at the same time. My head was pounding harder and harder. I was feeling scared and frightened. Then I cried out, "Jesus help me!" and I had no longer had said the words, when all of a sudden, the voices were gone. I could sense them still there, but moving away quickly. Fleeing like a mist being swept up, out to sea by a strong wind, and then, in a moment's time, I felt at ease. I had peace again. I could sense that the voices were not far away. They had gone some distance, then they stopped and seemed to congregate, waiting for something. I couldn't see them, but there was no doubt in my mind that they were there, and this was real.

Wednesday night had arrived and I was really looking forward to the church meeting. I pulled up in the car, parked and walked in with some others that were there for the meeting as well. The pastor greeted me when I walked into the building, shaking his hand and then being introduced by him to the others. As the meeting was getting under way I took a seat in the third row from the front and settled in for the class. The study was from the Bible, out of the book of Ephesians, and he was talking about spiritual battles. He shared with us the difference between the spirit life and the life of the flesh or the soul. Furthermore, he went on to tell us that these two, the spirit and soul, will battle against each other, and that the battleground was our minds. I instantly recalled that this was exactly what had been going on with me only two nights ago. I had been in a spiritual battle. *This was making sense to me now,* I thought.

I was attending the church meetings regularly and soaking up all I could learn. I wanted more and more. If I wasn't at Church I wanted to be there. Things at home were being stretched. I knew that I was living in a relationship that was not pleasing to God. It wasn't that there were any problems however. Diana and the kids were great. I have to admit they seemed a little puzzled by the changes in me, and who could blame them. I was behaving different than I had a few weeks ago. I was acting off the wall. I had met Jesus, and I thought that everyone should feel the same way I did. I was sharing my faith from a position of judgment, telling of the wrath of God, hell and brimstone. I wasn't sharing the love of Jesus, the peace. I wasn't telling them of God's grace, and what it was that Jesus did for mankind on the cross. I was sharing my faith from the place I was at when I got saved, out of fear. I was scared, and that is what caused me to turn and call out to God. I had this backwards, and instead of sharing God's grace and of His love, I was telling them of his punishment and making them to feel condemned. I was passing judgment on those I loved and didn't even realize it.

I moved out of the house, the warmest and most loving place I had ever lived in my life. I continued experiencing some heavy spiritual battles day and night. I had only been saved a few weeks and I was under extreme spiritual attacks, so I moved in with a friend. At one point while praying to God, I told him that I hadn't signed up for this. I was overwhelmed at times, and my legal situation added to the problem. I was saved and wanting to serve God, and at the same time, I was a fugitive, wanted by the law. I was calling myself a Christian and deceiving people about my true identity. I was even justifying my false name, telling myself that I wasn't the same person I was back then. I had a new start and a new name. Nothing else mattered.

I wasn't feeling any better about the way I treated Diana. She had uprooted her life and her children and moved here with me on the toss of a game board piece. How crazy it all seemed. How quickly life can change. I had experienced the presence of almighty God. This was not some figment of my imagination, something I had made up, or created on my own. I was smarter than that. I wasn't going off the deep end. I wasn't stupid. I had met Jesus, simple as that.

Chapter 41

The Vision

I enjoyed Sunday mornings so much. Seemed that I couldn't get enough of being in church and listening to what the Pastor had to share. I was even taking notes and writing down everything he had to say. I admit I loved going, and if I wasn't in Church I was thinking about being there. My mind was full of God and Jesus all the time. This was all I could think about. I had a new life and wanted to absorb all I could of what I was being taught. I was consumed with God and wanted nothing more than to please Him.

I was invited to have dinner after Church at the home of some very nice people I had met a few weeks ago. I felt a little uncomfortable at first when they asked me, but that soon past and I accepted. I hadn't been invited to anyone's home since I was saved, but now sitting there in their living room I was made to feel right at home. The home was very cozy and well kept. On the walls were hanging many lovely family pictures in nice frames. It appeared to me that the man's wife was a collector of picture frames. Each one was unique and beautiful. I was sitting on a way too comfortable couch and we were visiting back and forth with the ladies in the kitchen. The place smelled real good with whatever was cooking in the oven and my appetite was ready to be satisfied, and soon. I was about to doze off and caught my head falling forward a time or two, only to yawn and sit up straight.

All of a sudden I found myself in a vision or trance of some kind. I was standing at the bottom of a ladder that led up to the hayloft in a large barn. Standing next to the ladder was a man who I recognized as one of the Elders from the Church. He looked at me and motioned for me climb up. I took hold of it and climbed the steps to the top and stepped off, standing there for a moment. Then I heard the voice of God telling me to turn and look to the right, but for some reason I turned and looked to the left instead. What I saw there troubled me greatly. There was a clothes line stretched from one end of the hayloft to the other, and hanging from it was a full set of clothes. There was a shirt hanging from the line held by two clothespins and a pair of pants pinned to the shirt hanging down. It appeared to be like the form of a man blowing violently, whipping in the wind back and forth, to and fro in the middle of a severe thunderstorm. The sky was pitch black, the wind was extremely cold and I began to shiver. The heavy dark clouds rolled quickly through the heavens. The bolts of lightning were flashing electricity in every direction, lighting up the sky, and shooting bolts of light across the heavens from one end to the other. The thunder was piercing and extremely loud. I stood there frightened and scared as I was looking on.

Then all of a sudden I turned and looked to the right in the direction that I was told to look at the beginning. There I saw open before my eyes many rolling hills and fields of ripe golden wheat, corn and barley, glimmering in the autumn sun. It was swaying back and forth as a soothing and gentle breeze blew across the tops of endless, rolling hills. The sun was warm and the wind blew gently on my face. The sky was decorated in stunning colors of pastels, soft orange, red, and violet. The clouds moved swiftly through the heaven. They were large, fluffy white, beautiful clouds unlike anything I had ever seen before.

Then for a moment I attempted to open my eyes, but being heavy they were closed again. I appeared to be standing outside of one of the cheese caves carved into the cliffs back in Minnesota. The large double oak doors to the caves had been refinished. They were stained and polished, looking as beautiful and brilliant as the day they were made many years before. All of the other doors beside them looked old, wet and weathered and falling apart. Then suddenly I was told to open the new nice looking, well kept door. Stepping forward I unlatched the bolt pulling the door open. Gazing forward and peering inside I saw that cave was extremely deep, dark and cold. The breeze that came from the inside was chilling. As it blew past me I started to shiver from the cold air. Then in an instant I felt my head drop forward for a moment and the forward motion startled me. I was now wide-awake as

I sat up. I thought for a moment that I had fallen asleep and apologized to my host. I thought it odd when he told me that I hadn't fallen asleep. In fact he had been sitting in the chair right next to me. Then the thought had come to me that I had seen a vision.

Thoughts of my vision experience were on my mind continually for days. I was trying to understand what it was that I had witnessed. I wondered what it was that God was saying to me, and I felt somewhat weird thinking that this was real and that God wanted my attention. However what I had witnessed was so real and I needed to talk to someone about it. So I made up my mind that I would go and talk to the pastor and share with him what I had experienced and what I had seen.

The pastor was a nice man and I had become fond of him in the amount of time I had known him. I remember thinking to myself once that I could see the love of Jesus in his eyes. He had a real sense of peace that shined from him and I had grown to respect him a lot. There was of course the fact that he didn't know my real name, however those thoughts were becoming more distant by the day. So sitting there in his office I explained what I had experienced. The pastor said that it sounded like I had heard something from the Lord and he asked me to go ahead and share it with him. And so with that said, I began at the beginning and told him everything I had seen. When I was finished talking we sat there for a moment not saying anything and then he began to speak. He said that the vision in the barn was simple. The clothes on the clothes line blowing in the storm was me and what my life would be like if I turned from God and chose to walk in disobedience. On the other hand he said, the rolling fields of grain blowing in the autumn sunshine would be my part of the harvest of souls for the Kingdom of God as I walked in obedience. Talk about mind boggling! I was overwhelmed with the thoughts going on in my head, knowing that God had a plan for my life and that He could use me somehow. That I was called to be a son and a child of God to do His will in my life. Then I thought *what about my legal mess*? *Would it ever be over*?

"Please God," I said, "Use me to do what it is you want me to do with my life. Amen."

Chapter 42

Coming Clean

Wintertime in Washington was sure different than what I had been used too; rain, and more rain. *Would it ever stop*? I thought. It was a Sunday night and I was sitting in church, when Diana came and sat down beside me. I was sure happy to see her and she was looking good as ever and her smile was as warm as always. She said that she had something to share with me. She had been saved and accepted Jesus in to her life. This was great news! I was so happy for her. She explained that she now understood what it was that I had been trying to explain to her. She and William had been coming to church faithfully for months now, even though we hadn't been living together. This was so exciting for all of us and there was no doubt that God was working in our lives.

We began to spend more and more time together again. I had missed her, however we felt that we had to live our life right, and so we continued to live apart. There were some challenges being with her that were more physical than anything. Some days we were able to overcome them and then there were those when we didn't. I would find myself in a battle of doing what's right or of doing what's wrong. Then later in the night repenting for my behavior, I was in the battle of the flesh and the Spirit. My will versus God's will. I remembered the Bible verse in John 3:3, "I must decrease so He can increase." I wanted to live like this, but I was having such a difficult time doing so. Denying myself was not easy.

One afternoon I had received a phone call from one of my friends at church telling me that some young men had come into his gun store wanting to buy a gun. They had reported to him that one of their friend's mother's boyfriends was an ex bounty hunter. They went on to tell him that they wanted a gun for protection against him. Well I admitted to myself that this was not a good situation and couldn't get the thought of it out of my mind. Stacy was, I'm sure, wondering what had happened to her life and to the rest of us too. Our lives had really taken on some changes in the way we lived and behaved. I was somewhat radical in my opinions and even critical at times, not always using wisdom or good judgment. I thought that everyone should be like I was in my new found hope and life in Christ Jesus. I didn't give thought to where others were in their life and was not realizing that my approach to sharing the Gospel was at times overbearing and sometimes judgmental. I didn't consider that when I was sixteen I had made some poor choices and run away too. So I decided to go and talk to Stacy and apologize and ask her to please come home.

That afternoon I kept thinking about this. It was all that was on my mind. Then I decided to go and deal with it before some young man got stupid. I drove over to the house where they stayed and went crashing through the door looking for the guy with the gun. One of the guys got mouthy with me and stood up to face me so I busted him upside the head. Then he tried to call the police and so I grabbed the telephone and yanked it out of the wall and left.

The next day I was staking out the house watching for the guy that wanted to buy the gun for protection from me. I had been there for about two hours when he came walking down the street. I timed his steps so that when he got close to my car I got out and said, "So you want to shoot me," and I fired him up. I punched him a few times to give him some education. "I am the guy you want to shoot, you little punk." I was confident that I had changed his mind.

Later that day I drove out to the ocean feeling guilty that I had slapped this guy up, at the same time I was also agreeing with myself that he got what he had coming. How dare he think he was going to get away with wanting a gun to use on me? And once again the battle broke out in my head. So sitting there in the car looking out over the ocean I broke down weeping and began to repent, asking God for His forgiveness for what I had done to this guy. I had fallen back in to my old ways to never let anyone threaten me, and I wept and wept for what I had done. I had sinned and the feeling was ugly. I hated it. I had given away my freedom.

By the time I got back to town the police had already been looking for me and so I went and informed Diana of what had taken place. She was not pleased about the matter and gave me some scolding. She suggested that I go get some rest somewhere and see her after she was off of work. We agreed on a place and time. We talked for hours that night about everything we could think of. Where we were and where we had come from. Furthermore we talked about where we wanted to be. Then I asked her for a second time if she would marry me, and the answer was the same as it was the first time, "I will marry you when you have your real name back."

We agreed that evening that it was time that I put all my trust in The Lord and come clean about everything, I needed to go and talk to the pastor and Diana said she would go with me.

Sitting there in front of the pastor I really didn't know what to expect. I told him that what I had to share was in confidence and he said, "If that is what you want, that is the way it will be."

I said, "Pastor, my name isn't really Tim Dunn."

He said, "Well what is your name?"
I said, "It is Chuck Dudrey."

"Well then I'll call you Chuck," he said.

I was somewhat surprised in his response. He was cool headed and laid back, and the news of my identity didn't even faze him. Then the Pastor asked what else there was that I wanted to share with him. Diana and I sat there and shared everything that had been going on and how it was that we had come to live in Washington. We talked for over a couple of hours or more before finally leaving. I decided then that having a clean heart with our pastor would be a way of life from now on. It was good to be clean.

That Sunday night I asked my pastor if I could address the congregation and ask for their forgiveness for the deception I had been living under. All of these people were so real and caring for Diana and me, and I love being there with them. I truly felt at peace and at home in the church. The pastor so gracefully set the stage for me to come forward. He explained that I had something of importance that I needed to address with them. And so I explained everything. I told them the story from start to finish, and that I would now do whatever it took to straighten up my legal situation. At the end of the Sunday night service each and every person in that church came to me and thanked me and extended their hands to me. I was grateful and I was free from the deception.

Chapter 43

What Is Your Real and True Name?

There was a warrant out for my arrest in town because of my kicking in the door and assaulting the two guys earlier in the week. Seemed that the law had a good idea who I was, so Diana, William and I took a trip to Northern California to do some relaxing and some talking about where I would go from here. We needed some time of refreshing to get our thoughts in order, and we needed some rest as well from the emotional roller coaster ride I had caused us over the last few months. I really didn't feel good about slapping the guys up, but I was still justifying it in my mind. And then the battle would rage in my head, back and forth, back and forth. Part of me had no problem with what I did, yet I had come to a place in my life where I wanted to think about what was right. I wanted to be the compassionate more caring person that I was capable of being, the man that God had changed me into. I had been freed from the old man when I accepted what Jesus had done on the cross for me and I knew it, but I continued to want to do things the way that I knew were wrong. Then I felt bad for them and knew that I would be asking them to forgive me for what I had done. God could change this matter into something good. Yes, I would tell them that I had been wrong, that I was sorry. It was interesting how my life had changed since coming to know Jesus. My thinking was not so much about myself and what I wanted to do, but more and more of what God would have me do. I knew that Minnesota had a warrant out for me too, so I thought that I would leave the matter up to the Lord. Yes, that was exactly what I was going to do. I had read in my bible something that caught my interest. "The battle belongs to the Lord." I hoped that I could remember that. I was in a fight that didn't even belong to me.

The plans were all taken care of and Diana and I were going to be married in a few days. I had decided to stay out on a small piece of property we owned until after the wedding. The place was only a mile from town and it had everything one could need, and the police wouldn't look for me there. So I spent my time there praying and seeking God on the matter of the legal problems I was having. It was most interesting that I wasn't having the intense spiritual battles like I had had only a few weeks earlier. I had made my mind up to trust the Lord. I had thought about the matter in some depth one night and came to the simple conclusion that I had trusted God to save my soul from hell, and to forgive me of everything I had ever done in my life. What a refreshing thought. I was not guilty in God's eyes for anything I had ever done. This alone was enough to rejoice. There had been some ugly stuff too. Not only were there the things people knew about, but there were the secret things, those things hidden that no one knew about, stuff the law wouldn't charge me with, crime I had gotten away with. Everything was forgiven, every single thing. The bible says that my sin was as far as the east is from the west. This was most comforting for me. I knew that I would spend eternity with Him in heaven, and so I decided I would trust Him in this small matter. After all, He is God.

Our wedding day had arrived and everyone we had met in Washington was there. I was really excited about what we were about to do. My dad had flown out to be there and was doing the picture taking and Stacy had come to support us and be in the wedding. We were so blessed to have her there with us. Everything was in order and my heart was pounding like crazy when the music started to play. I walked to the front of the church and stood in the same place I had only a few weeks earlier asking forgiveness and explaining my situation before the congregation. And now I was standing there at the altar waiting for my bride to walk down the aisle. William was standing next to me and so was our friend Ed who we had met since moving to Washington. He was my best man. Then Diana came walking down the isle and stood next to me. She was sure looking beautiful and I thanked God for her right there one more time. My heart was full of so much love and emotion that I was about to burst with excitement. Then the pastor started the ceremony, we said our vows, and fifteen minutes later we were married.

My life had never felt as complete as it was now. I was married to a lovely woman and the kids were as much a part of my life as my new wife. I had loved them both ever since we first met. They were my family and I had never thought of them any other way. My relationship with the Lord was growing daily and my legal issues, well, I really hadn't given them much thought.

I was finishing up from mowing the yard when a police car pulled up and an officer got out to talk to me. I had seen the guy many times before because he was our neighbor who lived up the hill from us. He said that he needed to talk to me because there was some concern as to my true identity, and that he had a warrant for my arrest for assault. As I was put into the back seat of the car I began to pray in my heart and ask the Lord to protect my family. I said, "Lord, you are God and you can do anything. Please help me through this trouble, and help me to rely on your strength open my eyes to see this situation through your eyes."

I was led to a holding cell and the door was closed behind me, and I began to pray some more. I was praying out loud now and asking the Lord to guide me through the next few days.

"Father God," I prayed, "whatever it is you want of me I will do,"

Then the officer returned and asked me some information and wanted to know my real and true name. I told him and then he asked for my birthday and left. Then I continued to pray some more. I knew that there were those in Minnesota that were mad at me for not returning to court and I prayed for them.

Then all of a sudden my heart was still and my mind was at ease as the Spirit of the Lord spoke to me and said, "As I set Peter free, I will set you free also."

I was amazed once more that I had heard from the Lord. I had no longer finished hearing this when the officer returned and said, "Minnesota called us and said that they don't want you anymore, and told us to set you free."

He continued to let me know that I had to face the assault charge here in town, but I would be out of jail with in an hour. Then he said something interesting to me. "I have been in law enforcement for twenty years and I have never seen anything like this happen before." I continued to praise God some more. Yes, I was free.

Chapter 44

Men's Accountability Group

One year ago I was sitting in the King Dome in Seattle, Washington with tens of thousands of Christian men praising and worshiping God, the place was packed. This was my first time attending a Promise Keeper's Convention, and what an experience. Many of the men from our local church had been encouraged by our pastor to attend, and I was not so sure that it was something that I really wanted to do. Well, I did end up going thanks to the persistence of my friends Dan Simons and Dave Bordner.

The topic that I remembered the most, or at least got the most out of, was when the speaker talked about men's accountability groups. This was something that I had been hearing about over the last few weeks, and it sounded like a real good idea, but I didn't have time to go out every week for men's group meeting. Dan and Dave were understanding about this and made the suggestion that we should hold the gathering at my house, and then I wouldn't need to go out. *Tricky guys* I thought, and so that is how it all got started. Every Thursday evening Dan, Dave and some other men showed up at my house for our weekly meeting. My wife would welcome everyone in the house and offer the guys some coffee and fresh baked desert. Then she would excuse herself and go to another part of the house and leave us to our meeting. We all took turns each week bringing something to eat and we made good fun of it. Dan's wife made the best pie, hands down and Dave, being newly married, got some good teasing.

In the beginning few weeks of our meetings we made some small talk, had prayer, and shared some of our testimonies. One man would share each week until we all were through telling our own story of how we had come to accept Jesus as our savior. It was surprising to me how much we all had in common, and still the events of our lives were so much different. When we had all told our stories and had gotten to know one another better, developing some trust and relationship, we started to discuss the importance of confidentiality. We all agreed that we would not share with anyone outside of our group what we had discussed. This gave each of us a safe environment to talk about the trials and issues we had in our lives, and to open it up for the more sensitive areas of our life, the kind of things that one wouldn't share anywhere else other than a protected setting. We would talk about men's issues and the struggles we had in common. We were beginning to cross a threshold where trust was honored between us and doubt was eliminated.

As time went on we were growing closer and closer as men of God, brothers by our calling and friends by our choice. I had matured so much in the last year in relationship with these men, and had accepted the fact that I needed men in my life I could trust, someone I could pour my heart out to. I found comfort in the fact that no matter what I was struggling with, or how ugly the sin was, I could count on my brother's support and encouragement. One of the best decisions I have ever made in my life was to give my brothers Dan and Dave permission to speak in to my life about anything, anytime. This was a bond that we all shared and it went both ways. I have to admit that there have been some times when it wasn't easy to hear what one of them had to say to me, but never have I ever regretted something they said to me or the permission I gave them to say it.

Brother Dave had missed the past two meetings because he had been out of town working. It was fire season and so that could take him anywhere. He worked for the Federal Government in forestry. So we were happy to see him tonight and to hear about what he had been doing. Dave told the group that he hadn't been feeling well, and while he was away working he was feeling sick. He told us that he had made an appointment to go to the doctor and would be going in a few days. We ended our group that evening with prayer as always and prayed for Dave and his health. Dan, our wives and I would all be going with him to the appointment in a few days.

Well the news wasn't good. Dave had prostate cancer and it was a quiet ride back home that afternoon. I have over the last years come to know the truth that Jesus not only died on the cross for the forgiveness of our sins, but that He also bore the stripes on His back for our sickness and diseases so that we were healed. So we prayed and fasted for many weeks on behalf of our brother. We believed that God could heal Dave of his sickness and I was looking forward to the day when we could praise God for what He had done. There were gatherings at Dave's home and we would all be there praying and trusting that he would be healed. Dave had only been married about a year when this all took place so there were some real hard times.

Dave continued to fail in his health. It was to the point that I found it hard to even go and see him. Before his cancer, Dave was a tall, handsome man that stood well over six feet and weighed somewhere in the two-twenty range and carried himself real well. But the cancer was destroying his body. He was dying right before our eyes, and to see what the cancer had done to him was heart breaking. We continued to have our group, but things never did seem the same without him. He became weak and frail. Then one morning he went home to be with the Lord. Part of me was so sad at the loss of a dear friend and yet, I was happy to know that his suffering was over. Dave was truly in a better place now. There would be no more suffering where he is. Dave was at the feet of Jesus.

Now today my brother Dan and I are still good friends. I would say that we are lifelong friends. We have been in fellowship now for over fifteen years and I expect that our relationship will only continue to grow get richer. Having a true friend that I can trust and turn to has made my life richer, and helped to be a better husband, father and a better man.

Chapter 45

Bumpa

It was sure good to have Stacy back home. The Navy seemed to have been good for her. If nothing else, she had met her husband there and now they had a little baby boy named Connor. It would work out well having the Stacy her family at home living with us. We sure had plenty of room in the large house and with a little rearrangement of the bedrooms and some furniture, they would feel right at home. We could help them while they got their feet on the ground, and started going to college.

It sure didn't take long for me to love that little boy. What a joy he was to have in our home and any opportunity I had to pick him up, I did.

When my daughter Jacqueline was a small child I went to prison for three years and I missed the opportunity to share my life with her. It was something that I had really missed, watching my daughter grow when she was a small child. And when William and Stacy came into my life they were both in Jr. High School, so I took a real fond interest in Connor. While the kids were gone to work or school, I took care of the baby every day. I changed him and fed him and anything he needed. I was there for him. I enjoyed walking around carrying him and showing him things. This was a new experience for both him and me. I would let him touch and rub the leaves on our herb plants and then he would smell them. Every chance I got to show him something different I did and I tried to make every moment we had together a learning experience for him.

The first quarter of college was about to wrap up, so the kids had made plans to go on a trip to Mexico for a week. They asked if I wouldn't mind watching the baby while they were away, and I readily accepted, I would love nothing more. This little boy had touched my heart in so many ways already and I was so thankful that God had given me this opportunity in my life. The first few days went as smooth as could be expected. He was starting to crawl and discover things on his own, pulling himself up and standing next to the coffee table. It was exciting to see how bright he was and how fast he was learning, and I was learning too, that was the reward. I did everything I could to care for him and keep him safe and I enjoyed being on the floor with him. My wife had to gently remind me more than once that she knew something about raising a child and he was her grandson too. So I would yield and she held and played with him too. We spent some very enjoyable evenings in the living room babysitting together.

Early one afternoon I was sitting in the recliner chair with my feet up on the footrest and the baby was lying with his head on my knees while on my lap. I had fed him and changed his diaper, and so now I could "goochie-goo" him, tickle his belly and play some peek-a-boo. We would sometimes sit like this for a couple hours at a time doing this. He would look at me with his little blue eyes and I would rub his cheek. He would laugh and smile, and he was making noises with his mouth now trying to say words. I was having the time of my life. This was pure joy knowing and caring for him. I would pray every day asking God to watch over him and to protect him. I prayed that no harm would ever come to him and that he would one day come to know Jesus like I did and one day call Jesus his Lord. And as we sat there enjoying the intimate time together, he looked up at me and called me Bumpa. Where this came from I had no idea, but throughout the day he kept saying it. Bumpa. This was now my new name, and I would grow to love and cherish it.

Except for Connor and me, the house was empty. Stacy and Brian were still on vacation and Diana was working. Connor was crying so I changed his diaper thinking maybe he was wet or even something worse and that would quiet him. Crying and more crying, I held him and patted his back thinking he might need to burp. That didn't seem to be the problem. So I started walking around the house talking to him, trying to comfort him, and he yelled and cried all the more. "Oh, little kid you're okay. Bumpa's here," I comforted. "It will be alright, it's okay to cry."

I sat down in the recliner and pushed the leg rest out and lay there holding him. He was looking into my eyes as to touch my soul, and at that moment, I heard the Spirit of God speak to me, and say, "Why don't you love me the way he loves you, and depend on me like he depends on you?"

All of a sudden I started to cry along with my grandson. I began to weep and ask God for His forgiveness. We were crying, this little boy and I. He and I all alone sharing a moment that would forever change my life. And then, like a storm that was over, we cried no more and went to sleep.

Chapter 46

Deception and Division

It would sure be good to move and get settled into our own hotel. I could knock the dust off my feet and find some peace again. The last three years had taken its toll on me. Ever since I became a Christian I had attended one church and we were members there for years. We had grown so much over the years in the faith and our relationship with the Lord. I loved the leaders and all the people. So many of them had become so much a part of my life. They were my family as much as my friends. My brothers and sisters in the Church had walked beside me through some difficult and interesting times. The love and fellowship was so real and good. I learned something about what being a family was, and how to live in relationship with others. I had been baptized here and this is where Diana and I were married. I loved our church. Our son had met his wife Christy here and this is where they were married. Christy's parents and her brothers had all become good friends with our family. We had met many lifelong friends.

Then one day my life was impacted by something that I had never thought about, or thought possible. There was a division in the congregation. People were leaving and forming another church. Those that stayed were at odds with those that left. Somehow there was a void in my life and I found myself at times in a vacuum of thoughts and emotions. I didn't want to accept that this church split had taken place, and I was disappointed with the way it was handled. There was no doubt in my mind that these people loved God, however the thing that troubled me was that by not taking a side one way or the other, I was feeling all alone. I didn't want to go to church anymore and when I did, I couldn't get out of there fast enough after the service. The joy of going to church and worshiping was leaving me and I was so hurt that I wasn't even looking for a way to change the situation. I would be shopping in a store and people I had known for years would see me and turn the other way. I had done nothing to them. There were those that wanted me to engage in conversations that I knew were wrong, and so to avoid them I would walk away. I made some attempts to get the leaders on both sides to sit down with me and discuss the matter, but the meeting never took place.

I made a decision against my wife's better judgment and stopped going to church all together. We did go a few Sundays to other local Churches, however I never felt comfortable. So I figured I would serve God on my own. I could read my bible and pray at home. Well, it sounded good to me, however it didn't last long. When I accepted Christ I didn't smoke pot any more. In fact that evening on the waterfront I asked the Lord then to take away the effects I was feeling that night, and he did. I wasn't high anymore, and didn't have any desire for it. Really I was pleased to have that behind me. Then later on, maybe five years or so, I did from time to time buy a bag, smoke some weed and get stoned. I would stop by some friend's house and tell them about Jesus one week and not accept the offer to get high, only to go back a few days later and get stoned then. Here I was going back to the lifestyle that God had delivered me from. There were many times I would get stoned in the car on the way home after buying a bag, and then a few minutes later start to weep and feel guilty about doing it. So I'd throw it out the car window or wait until I got home and flush the weed down the toilet and then be mad at myself for doing it. There were times that I drove back to where I had thrown the bag out the window the night before hoping to find it. And then I was back to having the battles in my mind, only this time I knew that what I was doing was wrong but did it anyway, and my head would pound and my heart was in a state of hopelessness.

I was sure that God didn't want me smoking dope, but I kept going back to it. I started growing it in my garage or in the attic, justifying that there was nothing wrong with what I was doing. Seemed every time I had a few plants ready to harvest I would get paranoid, always looking out the windows, thinking the cops were watching me, then pull up all the plants and throw them away. I had become a prisoner and given in to the very things God had saved me from a few years earlier and I didn't even know it. I was denying the truth and trying to hide from it. I had chosen to live in a state of deception. One night I had gone to bed real late having been sitting up feeling sorry for myself. I knew what it was I needed to do, but I was feeling so much condemnation that I wasn't even praying anymore so I went to bed and sometime during the night I woke up from having a nightmare.

I was running as fast as I could to keep up with William and Diana. We were in an airport and they were ahead of me going to board the plane. I had to hide my pot before I went through security so I wouldn't get caught. So I went around to the airport lockers and into the men's room to stuff it into my shoe. I knew that I would have to hurry so I started running to catch up with the others. All of a sudden I found myself in a long dark tunnel. The faster I ran the further ahead of me they were, and then they were out of sight. I was looking everywhere and then looking out of the terminal window when I saw them. They were both on an airplane rolling down the runway, looking back at me from the window, and I was left all alone. Then I woke up. I had been dreaming. I was in a cold sweat and shivering. As I laid there in bed for a moment the Lord spoke to me and said, "Get up and write down what you have seen on a piece of paper." I jumped up out of bed and ran down the stairs looking for some paper, but I didn't find any, so I went back to bed and fell into a deep sleep.

After a year of smoking pot again I was convinced that I needed it. I could think better, have better conversations and work faster than when I wasn't using. I could even show you a verse in the bible where God made the herbs for man. I was letting myself be deceived and yet continuing to justify what I was doing. The one thing that would always come up was that it was illegal. That I couldn't argue about, at least very successfully. Then one evening I heard something on the news that caught my attention, medical marijuana. Yes, that was the answer and so I made it my mission to search and find a doctor that would give me a prescription. I called for weeks looking for someone, and then one day I found my new doctor. Oh yes, I could smoke and grow pot in Washington legally. I thought that this was the answer to my problems. No more did I have to worry about it being illegal. Yes, now I thought I could be back in favor with God. After all I was not breaking the law.

We had agreed that we loved the hotel and so we made an offer to buy it. It was a cozy little place and we could retire here, doing what we love to do, having guests, serving people and getting paid for doing what we loved to do. It had been our desire to own a bed and breakfast or a small motel, and then we found the hotel. The place was picture perfect, neat and clean, ready for us to take over. It seemed that every time I was about to cut a deal on the property something would come up and we would be back to square one. This went on for almost three months, then one day I worked out the details and we were ready to move in.

The moving date was set and we were all ready to pull out of the driveway for the six-hour drive to central Oregon. We had formed a caravan of sorts. I drove my pickup truck carrying my pot plants, my buddy Bob drove the moving van, and Diana drove her car. We were on the road.

Chapter 47

The Hotel and the Café

The hotel was situated on the Main Street of a small town in central Oregon. The population of the town was 168 people and the total number of county residents was under twelve hundred people. We moved here because the town was located on a tourist highway. In the summer time people from all over the world came here to visit and see the painted Hills and the high plains desert. And beside all that, it would be a great location for me to grow my medical marijuana and set up my growing room in the basement.

The hotel itself was a historic building and much of the original decor still existed. We would move into the owner's quarters on the first floor. The building had a full basement that ran the total length of the building, some eighty feet. The facility had been completely remodeled and I had finally made the deal to buy it. We had been dealing with the bank for two months and with two appraisers to make the deal work. I have made tough deals over the years, but this hotel, well it was the hardest one yet.

So with all we owned in a large truck, and the help of my buddy Bob, we were moving in. We were sure that this was the right move for us and we would be retiring here. After only a few weeks the hotel was really getting busy. We were full every night. Of course that meant cleaning rooms and doing the laundry. Man did we have laundry! It seemed that the washer and dryer never stopped.

Diana and I really enjoyed sitting on the front porch and visiting with our guests. I would bring out my guitar to play and sing the old songs and we all enjoyed the evening. We were happy to be here and things looked began to look real promising for us.

The winter had come and gone and we were now gearing up for what we expected to be a good season for business. My medical marijuana project was going well in the basement and I was having all I wanted to smoke. I had now become a proponent of medical pot and had joined many the online groups getting tips to grow it better and the latest scoop on the best type to grow for my back pain. We had been attending church on Sundays, but I never did feel at home as when we were members back in Washington. I missed the fellowship and the friends that we had made over the years. Things were different here and the small town caught us of guard. I had never been one to be a part of gossip and really couldn't recall having been exposed to it much. However here it was the way of life. Everyone was talking about everyone else. I was in somewhat of a culture shock, quite frankly, and couldn't imagine some of the things people were saying about one another. They were even gossiping in the Thursday morning men's group I had been attending at the church. I decided that I would not engage in any of it, but it was going on with every person in the town. I recall mentioning it once to someone and was met with the response, at least when their talking about me they weren't talking about someone else. Strange statement I thought.

Next to our hotel was a small café, the owner approached me one morning and wanted to know if I wanted to buy it. He said that he was fed up with the people in the town and wanted to sell and move on. I explained that I didn't have much capital on hand to make the purchase, but he continued to bring the matter up. I was trying to encourage him to stay but he assured me that he was moving and further more wanted out of town as fast as he could get out. Then one day I asked him how much he needed for the business, and when I realized that we could walk into a fully operational café with two thousand down, and that it included the entire inventory, I said yes. So we now had a food service operation for our hotel guests. I was feeling pretty good and proud of myself. We had now take possession of two of the nicest properties in the county. We cleaned and scrubbed the café from top to bottom and gave it a fresh coat of white paint. It looked clean and fresh and with the new curtains Diana made for the windows, the place was a show place. Things really took shape and soon we hired some helpers and opened for business.

Sitting at a table on Thursday morning for the men's breakfast at the Church the conversation was about a problem they were having in the community. Apparently one particular man was causing a great deal of trouble for the people in town. They talked about how he was scaring his neighbors and shooting guns over the heads of their horses and frightening them. It sounded to me like this guy was some piece of work. He was supposed to be cutting fences, damming up the water in the spring and that kind of thing. I personally found it odd to hear some of what the group leader was saying about it. He sure wasn't talking the talk of peace and love; instead he was joining in on the conversation. I was missing my church back on the harbor big time. I in all the years of Church life had never heard such talk from a pastor, it was not godly, and it was gossip, heart wrenching and evil. The thing I found odd was that I wasn't having the battles in my head over this. I heard what was going on and saw the way they were handling it and I simply shook my head, deciding that I wouldn't have any part of it.

Things were going great for us at the café and the Hotel. I was feeling pretty good about all the customers we had, we stayed busy all day long. The cash flow was sweet and we were making all of our financial commitments with no problem at all. One afternoon while I was sitting on a bench in the front of the cafe I saw a man standing on the side walk a crossed the street looking my way, so I gave him a nod and he in turn did the same back and then turned and walked away. The town was alive with people. There were some who driving through and not stopping so I had an idea; I went and got my guitar and started playing and singing songs right there on the side walk in front of the café. Soon people started to gather around and listen I invited them to come on inside, this was working well. After a few days' I started playing and singing inside too and I was even getting tips.

The man that had been standing on the corner continued looking my way trying to get my attrition every time I saw him so one day I invited him to come on over and have a cup of coffee and some pie on me. He accepted, and within a week he was there every day. He was a pleasant with the customers and he had even put on an apron and was clearing tables, the guy was having a good time and was entertaining to watch. One of my regular customers asked if he could speak with me outside and so I walked out with him to hear what he had on his mind. He told me that he and the other ranchers would not be coming back to the café as long as Robert was there. I asked him why and he said, "You don't know" I replied no I didn't. He told me that the man Robert I invited in to bus tables was the crazy man they had been talking about at the men's meeting. He went on to tell me that he was big trouble. My response to him was that as long as he behaved himself at the café, he was welcome to stay. This didn't go over well with the ranchers. I couldn't tell him he wasn't welcome anymore, that wouldn't be right; he had caused no trouble for me.

As the weeks passed the people in the community didn't approve of my position about Robert. I explained that he hadn't been any problem and their response was, "you wait and see" My wife and I had given him a room in the hotel to sleep while he was in town and Diana had even purchased him some blue jeans and a couple shirts. One afternoon I was headed to the café from the hotel after taking a nap and there was Robert in an argument with another man. I asked him what was the matter and he didn't respond, so I told him that he needed to take the yelling somewhere else. He didn't like what I had to say, but he did leave.

A few days later we were gearing up for the busiest business day of the year it was the town's yearly festival. We had hired lot's extra staff and set up a grill station outside on the lawn for the people that simply wanted a burger and a cool drink. We had everything in order for the next few days, and then Diana and I both got sick with the flu. In the afternoon we would go to the hotel and sleep and try to break the fever then get up and go back to work the dinner rush. We had slept all afternoon and it was now time to go close the café and do the nightly cleaning. I was still sick and hadn't broken the fever yet. I had taken some cold medicine and all that it did for me was to knock me out and cause me to want to sleep. So I got up and got dressed and encouraged my wife to stay in bed to sleep and I headed for the café. When I got outside there was Robert again on the side walk between the hotel and the cafe arguing with one of the young girls that worked for us. He had a hold of her hand and wasn't letting her go. I told him to knock it off and to release her hand, that what he was doing was inappropriate. Well, then he started yelling at me and was raising his voice. I was sure that everyone in the hotel could hear him and anyone that was sleeping was now awake, it was already after ten. But he kept it up and I appealed with him to go home and we would talk in the morning. I kept walking toward the café and he was walking beside me yelling at me louder and louder. I continued to plead with him to please quiet down, but he wouldn't have any of that. He was not getting in my face screaming at me and I finally convinced him to leave.

As he was walking over toward his truck and I was asking him what I could do to help him tonight. He continued making loud noise as he climbed on to the bed of his truck. Still yelling and screaming at me, talking bad about mom and using all that kind of language. Then he poured some gas from a gas can in to a coffee can and then jumped off the back of his truck in an attempt to douse me with the it. As his feet hit the ground I swung and hit him in the arm with my baton and broke it then he hit the ground. Next he got up off the ground and took off running and I gave chase behind him hoping to nail him again. I had had it with this character. Fortunately he was able to run faster than I was, so I went and finished up my work and went back to bed.

Chapter 48

The Longest Days

Seems that I had just gone to bed when it was morning already. The events of last night were still fresh on my mind and I was sick as a dog. I didn't want to hit Robert and truly didn't want to break his arm, however I wasn't about to let him or anyone for that matter, throw gas on me or attempt to hit me. I had seen that move before; first the gas, and then the Zippo lighter. The fact was clear and simple I thought, *You make a move on me, I nail you. Why do these type of guys always cross my path? All I did was offer the guy a helping hand.*

So I walked outside, headed for the café when I was approached by several of the men in town wanting to shake my hand. They were telling me that it was about time someone dealt with Robert. "Good job!" they were saying, "Sorry we missed it."

Well, it wasn't long and people were coming from everywhere thanking me for dealing with the town tormentor. They were giving me their phone numbers, telling me how glad they were that I had moved to town. I wasn't feeling so good about it however. I had liked the guy and was sorry that he pushed the matter.

"We could have told you there would be trouble once he started hanging around," they said.

Well I had wished that I didn't have to agree with them.

The town was coming alive in preparation for the one o'clock parade. We had the tables ready outside the cafe and were looking forward to a high cash flow day. As I walked back toward the hotel, two sheriff's deputies that wanted to talk to me greeted me. So I invited them into the hotel and we sat down to talk about the night before. The first thing the deputy said was, "Job well done." Then they went on to say they needed to hear my side of the story.

I simply stated that I had attempted to quiet down Robert who was acting crazy and hurting one of our waitresses. I explained that I walked over toward his truck and that he attempted to throw gas on me so I hit him as he jumped out of his truck with the can in his hand. Then I chased him down the street to run him out of town. Then the deputy wanted to know if I would let him see what was I was doing down in the basement. He told me that Robert had reported that I was growing marijuana down there. I said to him that I didn't have to show him anything without a warrant, but because I wasn't breaking the law, he was welcome to come on down. So I took him down and showed him my growing room of medical marijuana plants and there posted on the wall was my legal permit to grow my plants. As the deputy was standing at the front door of the hotel ready to leave, he turned and told to me that there was a witness last night that saw everything. He went on to tell me that the witness said that I had to have had the patience of Job in dealing with Robert. HE stated that he wondered how I could stand there for so long and take all the threats and insults for as long as I had the night before. As he left, he said that he doubted that there would ever be any charges filed.

A short time later I walked outside and there was Robert yelling and screaming again. He was telling everyone in town that I was growing pot for the cops and that they had paid me to beat him up. The street was full of people, but his yelling and screaming was turning them away from my business. He stood on the corner twenty feet from our café and yelled and screamed pointing his finger and the people walked away.

This went on for hours. We were losing business. The café was almost empty. I was beginning to have thoughts of another time and place, thinking how I would handle the problem. At this point I was all I could do to keep from going over and giving him some old school, knocking his head off. I hadn't felt like this for years. This had already gone on for hours and the sheriff's department did nothing. Finally about noon the deputy and his wife, who by the way was the festival director, tricked Robert to follow them in to the feed store. I don't know for a fact what they said to him, however my guess is that it was a threat of bodily harm. He left town for the day.

The next day the town was quiet, but the café was busy with people. All anyone wanted to talk about was the night someone finally dealt with Robert. This was the busiest morning we had ever had. Local people I had never seen before were coming in to thank me for what I had done. People were telling me their stories about Robert and that the law never did anything to stop him. This went on for weeks. Every day it was about Robert until I had heard enough. I was sick of hearing his name and didn't care if I ever saw him again. Then one day I received a letter from the Grand Jury ordering me to appear in the matter of the State of Oregon versus me.

I had met the County Attorney twice before in county business planning meetings. He seemed to be a rather nice man and I was sure that like the sheriff had said, I wouldn't even be charged. So sitting there I was given my rights and then they asked me questions. I told them the entire story from start to finish and then headed home, back to work.

For months the Robert saga continued. He took up residence, camping on the sidewalk across the street from the hotel. He was camping only a hundred feet from where I slept. During the night I would look out of my bedroom window and he would be standing across the street staring in our direction. When he saw the light go on he would move into the shadows. One day he brandished a firearm at me. I called the sheriff's office and reported what had been going on. The law told me that there was nothing that they could do. I said that he was stalking us and I wanted a protection order from the court. They stated that there was no such thing in Oregon. What was going on now with me was the same thing that he had been doing to the others in the community for years. The law didn't act. Then one day I was placed under arrest and was charged with assault. I really had had my fill. I wondered if Robert ever realized how thankful he should be to my wife for the protection she had afforded him from me.

Finally after over a year of this situation going on day after day, I had had enough. I told my wife on June first that we were moving, and putting Hell Town behind us. The Fourth of July, Independence Day, we were moving and never looking back. I was really in a life struggle. Fifteen years earlier I would have dealt with this worm with one swift move, but now I was a citizen. Let the law deal with it. I am a Christian, halfway anyway, and my wife was right. Leave room for God to work. Then that night I was awakened from my sleep and laying there in bed, I recalled the vision I had years earlier of the clothes hanging on the clothes line whipping and blowing in the wind of a thunder storm. And then I realized that it was me, living a life of disobedience apart from the will of God.

Chapter 49

Missouri Hide Out

With everything we owned in the back of a pick up truck and a twelve-foot u-haul trailer we were headed to Missouri. It was Independence Day. I was numb at the thought we had left everything we had behind and sold what we could, yet I was relieved to get away from the biggest mistake of my life. We sold the hotel on a contract and so I had hopes of recouping some of our investment. It wasn't the town or the people as much as the disobedience in my moving here. My motives were not pure and I knew it then. Now I was definitely reaping what I had sown. I was feeling sick and free at the same time as we pulled out of town. I wanted out of there so bad. The offer from the County Attorney to spend thirty days in jail was not good enough for me. It was the principle of the thing. They could keep their county and hell town too, as far as I was concerned.

We ended up in a small town called Ink, Missouri. The town had two houses. That's it, nothing else. We rented a house from a man that I was doing some work for. While the promise of work always sounds good, not having work, well, that is another thing. That winter I sold our pickup truck to make the rent payments and buy a computer. We spent the winter there and I finally accepted the truth that what I had been doing was not at all in God's will for my life. I was so far from where I had once been in relationship with Him. Every day since I had left Washington the Holy Spirit would prompt me. Still I was determined to do things my way. There was never a day that went by that I didn't know that I was living in the bondage of sin. I was a prisoner. The most startling thing about it was that it was all of my own doing. I made the choice to be where I was. One day I would pray and repent and ask for God's forgiveness, and the next day I would plan and do things my way all over again. I was living the life of a double-minded man and I knew it, yet I continued on my own path.

My wife was reading her bible and spending time in prayer more and more every day. I was to the place where I didn't even want to see her with the bible in her hand. I would walk past her and pretend that I didn't even see what she was doing. I would pray some sort of *think it would get me by* prayer, and continue to do what I was doing, thinking that I was at least getting by. Then one day Diana said that she needed to talk to me about something and wanted me to sit down.

I recalled, as I took a seat, what my Pastor had said to me years earlier. He said, "Chuck, you're like a large ship in the ocean and when you get going in one direction it takes a long time to get you turned around." He continued, "Large ships have a small rudder that controls their direction and can set them on a new course. Chuck your wife is your rudder, when she has something to say, you need to be still and listen."

And so with Diana looking at me the way only she can, she was giving me something to think about. Then she ended with, "You're my husband and my spiritual covering and you have holes in your armor. You need to get your life back on track." There was nothing I could say in return, she was right and I knew it.

We had made an investment a couple of years earlier that had paid off, and so we received a check in the mail for twenty-five thousand dollars and sixty-eight cents. We decided that we needed a car and a place to live and so we started looking for a house to buy. One day we drove to look at a house in the country and as soon as we saw it, we knew that it was what we were supposed to buy. We had agreed with the realtor to see him again after lunch and so sitting in the parking lot ready to go in, Diana said to offer low, real low. I was almost embarrassed at the price she said to offer, but I did as she asked and they accepted. We closed the deal on the spot. We were now homeowners again. We liked our little place, and part of the deal we made to buy it was that we offered the sellers one year's payments at closing in a separate check. They were pleased and so were we. The thought of no house payments for a year was sweet. Now we could work on our new home and relax for a while. The house was a small place thirteen miles from town. Interesting enough the name of the county was Oregon. We had five acres and plenty of room for our dogs. I felt better than I had in some time. The day we moved in a boy from down the road stopped by and invited us to come to his church on Sunday. I think he was surprised that I said we would see him there. Then, after I had promised him, I wished that I'd have kept my mouth shut.

That Sunday we walked in to a small country Church called Oak Hill Missionary Baptist Church. We were warmly welcomed by the pastor, as he introduced himself to us. This was sure different from where we had worshiped a few years ago. There was no dancing, clapping or anyone saying praise the Lord. The message was good and I found that I liked the pastor from the start. It was interesting that even though I was in an ugly sin state, I could recognize the Spirit of God all over him. The drive home to our new house was two miles. This suited me well. Things were looking up once again and I was going to church. I was feeling pretty good with myself.

May in the south is sure different than the northwest. People had their gardens in early April and were already eating fresh beans. I was enjoying living in the country. The deer were thick on our property, and so were the wood ticks. I had never seen so many wood ticks in my life. We had our garden plowed and planted and it was soon that we had fresh radishes to eat. The people at the church were the greatest. They were always stopping by with some garden stuff or fresh eggs for us, and we really felt welcome. Our prayer life had picked up and so was the time we spent in the Bible, however I was still smoking pot from my last indoor garden and I had already planted some plants outside for my for my next crop.

We continued to go to church and I had gotten a job working in a telephone call center. I was enjoying coming home after work and spending time in the garden and working on the house. I had to put on a new roof and at the same time we decided to rebuild the back porch area and turn it into a larger bathroom. I went to a sawmill and got all the lumber I needed for my project and so the work was coming along well. I was feeling pretty proud of myself the way thing things were going. Diana had started working for a social services organization and we were doing better than we had for the past couple of years. Then one evening I decided that I had had enough of marijuana and that it was time to quit for good. I took my pipe apart and threw the pieces in every direction I could. Then I called my wife and told her of my decision. While she was on the phone, I poured fuel on it and set it on fire, burning it all. I was sure that I was finished and thanks to God, I was.

My days of pot smoking were over. I had smoked pot for thirty years and gotten to the point that I didn't even like it anymore. I had had enough. I had smoked weed everyday all day long. It had become a religion and I didn't even realize it. I carried a pipe in my pocket and had a small tin that I would fill every morning before I had even had a cup of coffee. The marijuana use was a large part of the spiritual battle. It waged war against my spirit. Truth is that you cannot serve two masters, and I had allowed the drug use rule over me. There had been so many times that I had attempted to quit, and then I'd go and get some more. Many times I would throw it outside and then giving into the temptation, crawling on my hands and knees on the ground looking for it again to smoke some more. Before the pot growing days, I would buy some, smoke it and then feeling guilty, throw it out the car window or flush it down the toilet. And then I'd weep, calling out to God asking Him to forgive me. This type of behavior went on for years. I had justified my drug use to the point that I was an advocate for it, joining pro marijuana groups on the Internet. I joined the groups and the forums looking for the better strain to grow, wanting to have the best smoke. I wanted to grow the best and so I ordered seeds from overseas. I was so caught up in the lifestyle that it was all I wanted to think about.

Sitting at the table each morning with my wife, reading our Bibles and praying, had now become a way of life for us. I found that I could hardly wait to study. We studied every day, reading the word of God out loud. I love that verse that says, "Faith comes by hearing and hearing the Word of God." I suppose that is why we started reading out loud together and we have continued for years now, to grow our faith. This practice had become a way of life for us. We began to pray for those in Oregon that had caused us so much trouble. We asked The Lord to make the Oregon problem go away so that we would not have to be concerned about it any longer. We prayed for the county attorney and the sheriff and anyone else we could think about in the matter, that they would forget me.

We had joined the church we had been attending and were so happy to be back in fellowship with other believers again. The community we lived in was a small town of about seven hundred, and fifty or sixty of them were members of our church. I remember telling Pastor Edward that the Lord had given us the finest people in the county to be friends with. I think that every local church has its own uniqueness and for Oak Hill, it was most definitely the love for the brethren that shined bright. In the Ozarks people heat their homes with wood and each fall all the men would get together and cut firewood for those that needed it. If someone was hurt or off work for some reason there would be a food drive on Sunday night and we would deliver pick up loads of groceries to their house.

Everything a family needed to eat was in the trucks, Coolers of frozen meat, dozens of eggs and dairy products. This was a way of living in this small country church. The people were always looking for an opportunity to serve and help someone. We were so blessed to be a part of this way of life.

Then one afternoon looking out the front window I saw two police cars drive past the house. This was the first time I had ever seen a police car on our road and as I watched they went down the road and turned around and came back and parked in my driveway. I went outside as they came around the corner of the house. When they saw me I was asked if my name was Charles Dudrey and I stated that it was. I asked them to come into the house and as they did they said that there was a warrant for my arrest from Oregon. I thought to myself *well you have been praying that it would be over*. I asked the officers if I could change clothes and have a moment to pray with my wife and they said yes. And after being so kind to give us a few minutes together, they took me to jail. Oregon wanted me.

Chapter 50

The Oregon Trail

Walking into jail was not what I had in mind when I was praying and asking God to take care of my Oregon problems. But I have come to realize that God answers prayer His way and in His timing, and that He is always correct and perfect in what He puts His hand to. So here I was in another county jail, only this time I walked in carrying my Bible.

The first thing that always happens when you get to jail is everyone wants to know what you're there for and you're always sized up fairly quickly. Some things never change. It seemed that the other inmates already knew who I was before I even got there. I had been on the local radio station as the fugitive from Oregon, arrested at his home on numerous assault charges. So I settled in and got as comfortable as I could and tried to go to sleep. I had been in this situation way too many times in my life and each time it was going to be the last. *Right* I thought.

Later in the evening I called home and talked with Diana. I had never been in jail except for an hour or so in all the years we had been married, or known each other, so this was all new for my wife. My concern was for her more than anything at this point. She would be all right. I knew that. Diana was always on top of her game. And there was comfort knowing that my friends at church would look after her. Pastor Edward would help any way he could, that was one thing I knew for sure. He was a proven friend. As for me, well, my troubles would come down the road in Wheeler county Oregon.

From the way the arrest warrant read it appeared that Oregon District Attorney was angry at me. He had added some additional charges now. It wasn't any longer assault. It was assault in the first, second and third degree, and they added a theft charge too. I had no idea what that charge was about. A delivery of a controlled substance charge was added too. That was for sure made up. So I sat in jail believing that God knew what he was doing. That was a sure thing. I waited for my court hearing and thought I should fight extradition back to Oregon. If they wanted me that bad they would have to get a signed warrant from the Governor of Missouri. So sitting there in jail I began to pray and ask the Lord what it was He had in mind. So I prayed, *Lord, use me for your glory.* I spent hours at a time reading my bible and writing some letters. Then one afternoon a young man asked me what it was that I was reading about and so I shared with him that all things work for the good for those that trust in the Lord. Then I said, "Son let me tell you this now. God has me here for a reason and it could very well be you. Do you want to meet Jesus? Do you want to be forgiven of every ugly thing you have ever done or thought about in your life? Do you want to be free from guilt and the hurts and pain in your life?"

He said, "Yes I do."

Then, as I was about to pray for him, another man said, "Wait! Please. I want to get saved too. I want to be free!"

And so I prayed for them both right then and there, and they accepted Jesus as their savior. So then we had a church service right there in the county jail, praising and thanking God for saving our souls.

My pastor had been up to the jail to see me many occasions. One morning as I was waiting to go to court, Diana, my Pastor, and another brother were visiting with me in the hallway outside the courtroom. Then a man that had recognized me from being in jail together came over and wanted me to pray for him before he went to court. The Lord was keeping me busy in jail and so we were all thanking and praising Him right there in the courthouse.

When court was over it looked like I was going back to Oregon and so I got used to the idea. Now it was a matter of them sending someone to Missouri to get me. I had been in jail now for three weeks and Diana was sitting in the visiting room talking to me from behind the glass partition. While I was there a young man, may be twenty years old, was locked in the same inmate area as me visiting with someone too. We were now sitting there after the visitors had gone, waiting for the jailer to come and take us to our cells when I said to him, "Son, do you know who Jesus Christ is, and have you ever prayed and asked Him to forgive you of the sin in your life and to save your soul?"

He looked at me with tears in his eyes said that he hadn't.

I said, "Sir, you have never met me before and will never see me again after today, but listen now. This is the time to ask Jesus to save you. Are you ready? Don't pray because I asked you to. Pray because you want Jesus to save you from the sins in your life. Do you want Jesus to come into your life?"

"Yes," he said, and he was saved there on the spot, weeping, as God began to do a wonderful work in his life. Walking back to my cellblock I realized what God's timing was all about. Three souls were saved in that jail and God had used me to share the message of salvation that can only be found in His Son, Christ Jesus.

Three days later the sheriff from Oregon was there to take me back to stand in front of the judge for failure to appear in court. One thing I recalled from the bail bonding days was that judges are not happy when someone fails to appear in their court. So I was shackled and handcuffed, sitting in the back seat of a rental car headed for Oklahoma City to catch a flight back to Oregon to stand before the judge. But God wasn't finished working on my behalf yet. It so happened, that along on the trip with the sheriff was one of the county judges from Oregon and the three of us were engaged in some very interesting conversation on our way to the airport. We were talking about Jesus. When we arrived at the airport I had to run to keep up with the sheriff and the judge because I was still in shackles and handcuffs, and then, right then and there it occurred to me, the dream I had a few years earlier of me running through the airport. God had shown me the whole thing then, in every detail and now it was unfolding exactly as He said it would.

Chapter 51

Vengeance is mine

On the flight back to Oregon I had asked the sheriff if he could set up a meeting between the county attorney and me. He said that he would. I didn't have a bad relationship with the county officials in Oregon. In fact it was rather good. I had cooperated with them throughout the entire process up to my having to sit in jail. I attended the grand jury hearing without an attorney. I stated the truth then, and continued to do so. The sheriff even agreed that I didn't do anymore than he would have done. The thing that was hurting me now was my prior record of twenty-five years earlier, and now of course, the failure to appear in court. Interesting how the past is never far behind, no matter how much time has passed.

I had made my mind up many years ago at the top of the stairs that no one would ever lay a hand on me ever again. I still hold to that today, except for the times I was hired for pay, and that was business. I don't recall ever hitting anyone that didn't raise their hand against me first. Robert was the county troublemaker and I still don't think I did anything wrong when I hit him. His problem was that he moved on the wrong guy and he earned his reward. So sitting here in the courthouse, waiting to meet with District Attorney. These were the thoughts going through my mind as the district attorney walked in and we shook hands. We made some small talk and then he made it clear that I had ticked off the judge and that he had no other choice than to add charges to my case. And so back to the jail I went, waiting for my next court appearance. I had been sitting in jail now for over sixty days and was praying that this mess would soon be over.

Things were not looking that good for me. It looked like that with all the charges facing me I could serve one hundred and thirty months in jail if found guilty of everything. The court appointed lawyer was the same guy I fired three years ago in this same case. He looked like Opie Taylor and dressed like him too. He was one of those guys that never seemed to fit in. As he sat there behind the glass talking to me it was clear that he didn't really want to represent me. In fact it was obvious that he didn't like me. Two rules to live by with lawyers: One - they need to believe you; Two - they have to like you. If they don't all you get is the routine, go through the motion defense. I wanted to ask him some more questions and he flaked out on me. I decided then and there I would have to hire an attorney. This guy sat there and admitted that he already had fifteen more clients to see after me and that he wanted to get home. So I called Diana that night and told her the story. She agreed that we needed to hire an attorney, but we didn't have five thousand dollars. That evening I lay awake praying and thinking, and decided that in the morning I would call Pastor Edward.

Diana had flown out to Washington and talking to her on the phone she told me that she and William were coming over to see me and talk about my case. She also stated that before she left Missouri a man from our church came up to her and handed her a check for my attorney fees. She said that he told her to go Oregon and bring her husband home. Leave it to William. He had called and talked to the jail superintendent and arranged for us to visit in the lawyer's visiting room, and to have an extended visit as well. So we had all the time we wanted to talk. The visit was as good as a jail visit can be, but I was still convinced that I was going to prison. My wife reminded me to trust God and not myself. It was hard, I have to admit, but I had surrendered my life to Christ. I was His and not mine own any more. Seems that when things are good, praising God and calling on Him is easy, and then when you really need Him, you tend to rely on your own strength. Seems that I had it backwards. So as the visit ended, I made sure to send all my personal belongings home with Diana just in case.

One month later I was sitting in a holding cell early one morning waiting for the sheriff's deputy to come and get me for the long drive to court. Looking out of the cell window there was Robert being led in to another cell. *What was he doing here* I thought. It had been three years since I had seen him, thinking he hadn't changed much. For a moment my heart started to hate him again and then I remembered how I had forgiven him many months earlier sitting at the table at home. With this in mind I started to pray for him, asking God to heal his heart and that he would come to know the Lord. Then I prayed and asked God that my life today would bring honor to His name. When the deputy came, he told Robert that he had better behave on the ride to court and then he put him in to the police car. Next he came and got me, and now I was seated next to the guy that had cost me so much and who I had once hated. Now I am expected to love him? As it is written, love your enemies.

All the way to the courthouse I prayed for Robert. I wouldn't let the hate that was once there come back. I have to admit that I was sure this car ride was planned, having the two of us side by side for the sixty-mile ride to court. My guess is that back at the sheriff's office they were laughing about it, wondering if Roberts's mouth would be running, and if I wouldn't try to knock his head off.

When we reached our destination we were led to the holding cell in the middle of the sheriff's office. The entire sheriff's department was, I'm sure, waiting for Robert to start running his mouth and for me to knock his head off. I, however, continued to pray and asked God to reveal to me what he was doing here. Then after a while Robert started wanting to communicate with me. He was whispering and trying to get my attention, careful not to let anyone see him talk to me. This was the same behavior he practiced back in town three years ago. Robert was the sneakiest man I had ever met. He told me that if I would tell the judge that the sheriff's department had paid me to beat him up, that he wouldn't testify against me in court. He said, "Tell the judge that I was growing dope and the sheriff's department and they were in on it with me. I thought that perhaps he had become more delirious than he had been three years ago. He kept trying to get me to agree with him on something, to lie for him. I thought, *how dare you sit there and expect me to lie for you.* Then for a moment I felt sorry for him, recalling how I had once liked him and given him a chance, how we had tried to help him. But he wouldn't stop whispering. He told me how the cops had paid someone else to beat him up and showed me his bottom lip where the guy had bitten it off. He was almost begging me to help him to get out of his troubles, pleading with me for help.

The bailiff came and took us up to court. There we were, sitting side by side in court waiting for the judge to make decisions in each of our lives. Robert's turn was first. It seemed that he was continuing to do the same kind of things he did three years earlier, and now they were adding more charges against him for trespassing. Then it was my turn to stand before the judge, and I plead not guilty on all charges and was ordered back to jail to await trial. As we were led back down to the holding cell I mentioned to the deputy that I wanted to speak to the sheriff before I went back to jail. I told him it was important and he said he would pass the message on.

Sitting in the sheriff's office I recounted the remarks that Robert was making. I told him everything about how he wanted me to lie for him against the sheriff's office. I said that I didn't want to sound like I was making this up and lying and the sheriff said that he believed me. He went on the say that the only way I could possibly know about what I was sharing with him would be if Robert had told me. Seemed that the latest assault on him was while I was in jail and there is no way I could know these things on my own. Then before I left I said to the sheriff, "How convenient that Robert and I should be here together today."

He smiled and said, "Isn't it though."

All the way back to the jail the whispering continued. I wished that he would shut up, but somehow I knew this was part of God's plan, because it is written, "Vengeance is mine says the Lord."

It had been a week now since I was last in court and I had been called to go to the visiting room. Seemed that my lawyer was there to see me. When I saw the look on his face I knew that he had news for me. He told me that the county attorney had made an offer for me. If I would enter a plea of guilty to the charges, he would agree that I would only have to serve six months in jail, that he time I had already served would be applied, and so I would be out in about a month. Also, after I was sentenced, I would be required to testify before the grand jury in the matter with Robert. Seemed that he was now being charged with witness tampering. I was the witness.

Chapter 52

Going Home

As my wife drove the car in to the driveway the feeling of being home was good. I really liked our place here in Missouri and I had missed it on many days while sitting in jail. Now, with all that behind me, it was time to look forward to what we would be doing with our future.

As part of my plea agreement in Oregon I had to be on probation for three years and pay a lot of money for court cost and fines. So I set up a meeting with the probation department and went to meet my supervising officer. He was a likeable man and I thought it interesting that after reading my case file that he wondered out loud why I was even on probation. Interesting enough he asked why I had even been charged with a crime, a thought that I had asked myself many times. So after a good meeting I decided that I would like having this man as a probation officer.

All our friends were happy to see me, and it was a good feeling to be back in church on Sunday morning worshiping and singing songs of praise to Lord my God. There was no doubt that God's hand was at work in my life. There were simply too many things that have gone on that can only point to Him. God can take evil and use it in for good, and I am confident that is exactly what He did in Oregon. Even while I was in jail here in Missouri three people came to know Christ Jesus and I had the opportunity to pray for many more. Who would have guessed that the events in the sheriff's office would have turned out the way they did. God makes no mistakes, and to think otherwise is simply foolishness. He is in charge and He will use people and the situations in their lives in order for His will to be accomplished.

We had been remodeling our home and had come to the conclusion that God wanted us to move back to Washington. We missed our son's family and the grandchildren, and longed to be closer to them. So we continued to work on our property making it more suitable to sell. Diana had an opportunity to fly back to Washington for William's birthday party in December, and I am sure that it was then we realized that the Pacific Northwest was our home. When she came home from the trip all she seemed to talk about was being a part of our grandchildren's lives. So we put the *For Sale* sign out and placed an ad in the local papers. We were getting calls and people were looking at the house and a few really wanted to buy it. However, something didn't seem to be in place. We were not getting any offers.

In April, Diana got a call that there was a job opening with the company she had worked for a few years earlier, so she went back to Washington while I stayed to sell the house. There was a lady at our church that was a real estate broker so I enlisted her help. We had put ads in the paper, on web sites and yet we were getting no offers. So I continued to improve on our property and trusted that God had a plan. We would watch and see what it was He was going to do.

One evening I got a telephone call from a friend of ours stating that their dad was in failing health. He had been in the hospital off and on for the past few months so I went down to see him. Enos Hand was a lovely man with a gentle way about him and Diana and I had grown to love him and his family very much. We first met Enos while going to church. He was a godly man of over eighty years, who spoke with a gentle, soft voice mixed with a Missouri accent. Interestingly enough was the fact that he and his father's family used to grow sweet potatoes in the very spot where our house sat back in the nineteen forties. So we spent much time talking about those days, drinking coffee and eating homemade deserts from Diana's kitchen. I have to confess that I truly loved the man.

The doctors knew that Enos didn't have much time to live and so he was sent home from the hospital. When He got settled in at home I would go down to see him every day and visit. He would take my hand and ask me with his soft failing voice to pray for him. He said, "Brother Chuck please pray for my family, that they would all come to know Jesus," and so I did.

Holding his hand knowing that he was about to die was a numbing experience. I loved him and it was difficult seeing him like this. On Father's day, Enos drew his last breath and went to be with the Lord. I was sad seeing him lying there, and yet, I was full of joy at the same time, knowing this, that my friend was now sitting at the feet of Jesus, his first love.

Early on a Monday morning, eight days after Eros's funeral, I was going out shopping for a pickup truck that I would use to pull a trailer for the move back to the coast. I had planned to go to West Plains for the day to shop there. However, when I stopped at the stop sign about to turn in that direction, the Holy Spirit told me to go left. So I said *O.K. Lord, left it will be.* As I drove, I saw a truck for sale in a yard along the highway and thought this must be the one in God's plan. I asked *is this the one Lord*? and I didn't get a response so I continued driving. A few miles more I came to the intersection of another highway and was about to pull into the right lane when the Holy Spirit said, "Turn left." So I entered the turn lane and was on the highway toward Arkansas. I passed three more car dealers and heard nothing from the Lord. So I drove down through Mammoth Springs and turned into the first auto dealership I came too. They were closed. Getting out to stretch my legs and to let my dogs run there sitting up on a hill of the car lot sat a nice looking pewter colored quad pickup truck. I liked it the moment I saw it and walking toward it for a closer look the Lord said, "This is your new truck."

Placing my hand on the hood I said, "Thank you Lord."

On the way home that morning I was thanking God and praising Him for His faithfulness and love for me. I was amazed at the way he had led me all morning and it was not even nine in the morning. We always passed by the Hand's house anytime we went anywhere and today, was no different. So I pulled in their yard like I always did. Sitting on the front porch was one of Enos's sons and his niece, Enos's granddaughter was sitting on the steps. We greeted one another and then I sat down on the step next to the Ashley. I asked, "Is today the day that you're going to ask Jesus in to your life?"

She turned to me giving me a hug and said, "Yes it is Brother Chuck. I want Jesus to save my soul."

So sitting there on July 7th, I prayed with a nine year-old little girl as she gave her heart to Jesus and invited Him into Her life. I had no more than said *amen* when she jumped to her feet and ran into the house yelling, "I got saved, I got saved, I accepted Jesus into my heart."

Everyone in the house came running out to see what all the commotion was about, and Ashley kept saying it over and over again that she had found Jesus and that she was saved. This was Mr. Hand's final prayer before he drew His last breath, that all of his family would know Jesus. She was the last one, and God was faithful. He answered a dying man's prayer.

I got into my car and started to make the two-mile drive home. I had gotten less that a hundred yards down the road and the Lord spoke to me and said, "Now you can move, your mission here is complete." I had no more than got home when the phone started ringing. It was my real estate broker telling me that our house had been sold ten minutes ago. The buyers paid the full asking price and said that they would be moving in August first.

Chapter 53

The Little Ones

Really, I wasn't sure I could take another night of flashlight tag. I am after all still recovering from the night before of wrestling on the living room floor. Running in the dark at ten-thirty at night with two seven year olds and a three year old that would be nowhere else but in the middle of all the fun. It was, after all, two hours past my regular bedtime, I reminded them. "Let's go out now and play," I suggested earlier.

"We can't play yet, Bumpa. It is not dark enough out!"

So the time had arrived as I put on my shoes on for yet another time.

"Bumpa it's your turn. You're it!"

"You count to a hundred and come and find us."

And so I was it and taking my time counting. I needed to catch my breath.

"Bumpa we are waiting. Come and find us."

I was sure that they must have seen me coming. I was getting closer and about to close in on their position, and then they would run and hide again.

"I see you," I called after them.

"No you didn't Bumpa," they said. *I must be getting tired,* I thought.

Only an hour ago I was pleading with them to not jump on Bumpa's belly as all three of them were on top of me on the living room floor wrestling for the second time today already.

"Tickle me Bumpa, tickle me some more"

"No, it's my turn, brother," one of them said.

I was already tired and worn out from the day of fun I was having with my son's three children, the little ones.

It was forty-eight years ago when I was seven years old and having been almost killed on more than one occasion at the hand of an adult. It was now clear to me that God has given me another chance in my life to be seven again. I'm sure that someone could find it a little unusual for a man my size and age to be playing and wrestling on the floor with three little kids, or building a fort out in the woods, but I didn't care much about what someone else thought. I am so thankful that I have a family that understands me and cares enough to know the heart of Bumpa. The God I serve is so good to me and He has been faithful and true to His word. Spending time with these kids is some of the most rewarding and enjoyable time in my life, and by far the most emotional. It is only by the grace of God that I have a family today. It was only yesterday that I was thinking back to what a Pastor said to me eighteen years ago at a church meeting.

I was standing in the front of the church at the altar when he walked over to me. I had never met this man in my life. He knew nothing about me. Then he laid his hand on me and began to pray and prophesy over me. "Son, hear what the spirit of the Lord has to say," he said. "God wants to restore unto you what the moth and the canker worm has destroyed. He wants to heal you from all the pain and hurts caused by the hand of your father in your life."

I was in tears and became weak as I fell down to the floor. Then he said to someone, "Help him up. God has more for him."

I stood there with tears streaming down my face as he continued to prophesy. "God wants you to know that he has plans for your life and that he will give you a beautiful wife and a family to love and to love you." Then I fell down and began to weep with thanks and gratitude for what God was willing to restore back into my life.

I have been writing my life story for about two months now. Interesting how it came about that I should be doing this. It has been no secret that I have lived an exciting, sometimes ugly, life, and come from a violent back ground, to say the least. One morning a few months earlier my pastor and I were meeting for no other reason except to get together and visit over a cup of coffee. During our conversation he said, "Tell me your life story."

That took me a little by surprise, but I thought oh well, better he hear it from me than from someone else. So I shared with him where I had come from and the lifestyle I had lived. I was forthright in sharing that even as a Christian I had turned back to some of the old ways and had really made some messes. Then I was sure to share with him where God was in my life today and how thankful I am that God is faithful and wants to restore forgive us, asking that we trust Him. At the end of our meeting my pastor looked at me and said that he thought that I should write a book of my life.

"That is interesting," I told him. "My wife has said that to me before too."

And so having had a nice visit we parted and I drove home not giving the conversation much more thought.

"Bumpa, I want Tooty Fruity's for breakfast."

"Bumpa, I want Coco Crunch and cinnamon toast."

"Bumpa will you help me get dressed?"

"I'll be there in a moment, now you guys don't spill your milk. And no fighting amongst yourselves."

"Bumpa, will you please help me get dressed?"

I have to admit that there is no fonder joy in my life these days than when I am with my grandchildren. As I spend time with them I am constantly reminded of where I have come from and where God is now in my life. I also know that if it wasn't for the love of God and His grace, the life I am sharing with my little ones would never have come to pass.

A little three-year-old girl sitting on my lap wanting to have her Bumpa's help is pure joy for me. I was putting on her socks, and teasing her about having stinky feet. I was at the time, as so many others lately, taken back to my childhood and the contrast of the life of these little ones, and that of me and my brothers and sisters. Holding back the emotion, so I wouldn't hear "Why is

Bumpa crying Grandma?" from the lips of an innocent child. I continued to dress her and tie her shoes.

"I love you Bumpa," she said as I served her breakfast. And then I was reminded of the morning so long ago that Barbara was dressing my little three year old sister. She pulled her hair and said, "Stand still you little %$#@," and then she slapped her in the face.

"Now hold your foot still %$# you so I can put your *&^%$ shoe on you," twisting her arm and turning her around with force and gripping her small arm, digging her finger nails into her skin. "What are you crying for? Knock it off!"

These were the words coming out of her mouth, filled with hate, directed at a small child, whose mother only a few years earlier was shot and killed while she and her friends stood there looking on.

So with these thought going on in my mind I had to excuse myself from the room and go spend some time with The Lord, weeping and asking Him for some more of His loving mercy for my life.

Chapter 54

Where I am Today

Today we make our home in the beautiful Pacific Northwest at the foothills of the Olympic National Forest. My wife Diana and I are involved in the lives of our grown children and our grandchildren. We continue enjoying the love and fellowship of God that I believe can only be found in the building of relationships with people in the local church. I have been blessed with a second chance in life, and with a wonderful and caring family. I have the joy and pleasures of sharing life with so many wonderful people who have, through the last twenty years, impacted me greatly. My family is the joy of my life and the evidence of God's promise to me so many years ago. Standing there being prayed for by a man that had never met me before, listening to him prophecy over me as he told me of God's plan for my life, and of the family I would have.

Sitting alone at times in my thoughts, I can't help but marvel at where I have been in my life and all that I have experienced, the good and the bad. I have absolutely no doubt that God has had his hand on me through all the years of my life. How else is it that I am still alive. As ugly and unfortunate as some of my life has been, I am constantly reminded that God can take evil and use it for good. Knowing this, that His grace is sufficient, and that the greatest gift to me and to all mankind is the free gift of eternal salvation through Jesus Christ.

CPSIA information can be obtained
at www.ICGtesting.com
Printed in the USA
FSOW03n0323260116
16042FS